We've been struggling with organizational issues for years. Our discussions were often confused, occasionally emotional, and rarely decisive. [The Building Blocks Approach] brought everything into focus. It's not a rigid answer.... It's a well-structured process with a clear language that helped our leadership team come to consensus on a whole range of tough issues.

> Bill Wilkins
> John Alden Financial Services Corp.

NDMA provided a well thought-out philosophy of organizational structure, and a practical process for implementing that vision.

> David A. Hall
> Corning Telecommunications Products Division

THE RESULTS

Changing everyone's paradigm is tough work. This process provided a framework for effecting significant change.

> M. Brad Hall
> Koch Industries

The [Building Blocks] language itself is an enormous benefit. It's helping us clarify our boundaries, and improves our ability to discuss our business with our clients.

> Ron Pace
> U.S. Army, Fort Detrick

THE PROCESS

[The Building Blocks Approach] presents a process by which an organization redesigns itself. The effort is participatory but controlled, and is calculated to yield a technically good solution that has very strong internal support.

Mark Luker
University of Wisconsin at Madison

Once we adopted the [Building Blocks Approach] principles, we had a framework that provided a basis for any decision, defused the inevitable turf battles before they ever began, and accelerated our learning process in a way that probably could not have occurred otherwise.

John Benci
The Canadian Wheat Board

The [Building Blocks Approach] process forced us to specify our products and services, [and] our customers and suppliers for each operating and support organization within our [department]. This brought to light many of the inefficiencies that we had been struggling with and allowed us to deal with them.

William T. Houghton
President
Chevron Information Technology Company

Having the [implementation] process defined and facilitated freed our team to creatively define charters to best serve our clients and coworkers.

Preston Simons
Rush Prudential Health Plans

The Building Blocks Approach to Organization Charts

*an overview of the
science of designing healthy,
high-performance organizations*

by

N. Dean Meyer

The Building Blocks Approach to Organization Charts: an overview of the science of designing healthy, high-performance organizations

Meyer, N. Dean

Key words: organizational structure, organization design, organization chart, teamwork, reengineering.

NDMA Publishing
641 Danbury Road, Suite D
Ridgefield, CT 06877 USA

203-431-0029

ISBN   1-892606-17-8

Printed in the United States of America.

BOOKS BY N. DEAN MEYER

Meyer's Rules of Order: how to hold highly productive business meetings. 2001

Simple, pragmatic guidelines for holding highly productive business meetings.

The New Lexicon of Leadership: dictionary of terms used in leadership and organizational design. 2001.

A glossary of business terms that are critical to clear communications and clear thinking about organizations and leadership.

RoadMap: how to understand, diagnose, and fix your organization. 1998.

The fundamental systems within organizations, and how to plan a transformation to a healthy, high-performance organization.

Outsourcing: how to make vendors work for your shareholders. 1999.

A critical analysis of the claims of outsourcing vendors, a review of the real reasons for outsourcing, and an approach to managing vendors through (not around) internal staff.

Decentralization: Fantasies, Failings, and Fundamentals. 1998.

Why decentralization is so expensive and harmful, and how to get the benefits without paying the costs.

The Information Edge with Mary E. Boone. 1987.

How to find and measure the strategic benefits of information systems (with over sixty case studies).

To Darcy Lorette Meyer Dunaway
who teaches through action
the true meaning of family.

CONTENTS

ASSEMBLING THE BUILDING BLOCKS

HIGH-PERFORMANCE TEAMWORK

IDEAS TO ACTION

FIGURES

The Building Blocks Approach to Organization Charts

*an overview of the
science of designing healthy,
high-performance organizations*

FOREWORD: Why Structure Is Important

This book explains how to design and implement healthy, high-performance organizational structures.

Many people believe that organizational structure has little impact on the real workings of an organization. After repeated reorganizations which do little more than optimize the careers of the top few, folks have every right to believe that a restructuring is akin to rearranging the deck chairs on the Titanic! For most staff, work goes on as it always did, perhaps with a new boss to put up with, perhaps with new political tensions replacing old ones, but with little real change in what people do or how well they perform.

The truth is, structure is one of the most powerful drivers of organizational performance — its efficiency, effectiveness, quality, creativity, innovation, agility, customer satisfaction, and competitiveness. Structure is also a key element of people's job satisfaction, empowerment, motivation and commitment, work relationships, and teamwork.

Consider some of the symptoms of a poorly designed structure that should be familiar to anyone who has spent any time working in a corporation:

*   People are disempowered — turned into passive "robots" — when their jobs are designed around tasks or rigid processes.

*   People are given impossible jobs — e.g., when they're expected to be experts at too many things — where super-achievers break even and everyone else fails to meet expectations.

*   People are put in conflict-of-interests situations when their jobs ask them to pursue paradoxical objectives — like keep things running smoothly (maintain stability) and also invent the next generation (shake things up).

* People are pitted against one another — set up to fight — when their domains overlap or are unclear, or when one group is charged with controlling, disempowering, or harming another.

* Critical activities fail to happen when they're no one's job, or when they're everyone's job.

* People build self-sufficient empires — "stove-pipes" — when their peers don't see them as internal customers and don't freely join their project teams.

When things are not going well, it's all too easy to blame individuals for poor performance. But that may be missing the real problem. Even the best people will prove disappointing if structural problems impede their performance. Until structural issues are examined, one cannot really know whether individuals are at fault, or whether great people are being set up to fail.

In contrast, a healthy structure makes an organization highly productive and a great place to work.

The bottom line: Put great people in a dysfunctional organization and they'll fail. On the other hand, in a healthy structure, everyone has a chance to succeed.

Structure is one of the most powerful tools leaders have to improve organizational performance.

I hope this book helps you build the kind of organization everyone wants to work for.

PREFACE: Context and Content

To put this book in context, consider what it takes to build a healthy, high-performance organization.

There are five basic systems at work within any organization:

* **Culture:** the behavioral patterns (habits and conventions) and values generally adopted within the organization.

* **Structure:** the definition of jobs and the reporting hierarchy (organization chart), as well as the processes that combine people into teams as work flows across organizational boundaries.

* **Internal economy:** the way money moves through the organization and resources are managed, including the budgeting, chargeback, project-approval processes, and resource-tracking systems.

* **Methods and skills:** the procedures, methodologies, skills, and tools that people in the organization use to do their jobs.

* **Metrics and rewards:** the feedback loops that inform people about how they are doing in time to adjust their behavior, and the incentives for improving performance.

These five organizational systems work in concert to determine whether the organizational environment is productive or dysfunctional. A visionary leader addresses all five in a multi-year plan to build a high-performance organization.

Structure is just one of the five. But it is one of the most powerful — and one of the most difficult.

It's difficult, in part, because it's emotional. Structural changes affect people's livelihoods, sense of competence, and mission at work. Change processes, to be effective, have to be participative, fact based, carefully planned, and meticulously executed.

It's also difficult because structure affects people's working relations with peers. Structural change invariably changes who does what; it changes the way work flows across structural boundaries.

Another reason structure is difficult is that it's a complex topic. Designing a healthy structure is not a matter of drawing a few boxes on an organization chart. It's not a matter of personalities, politics, fads, and intuition. There are fundamental principles at work — a science of structural design.

To give you a taste of this science, there are five fundamental building blocks of structure present in any organization. The way these are combined into an organization chart determines its health and performance. And the mechanisms of teamwork (cross-boundary work flows) determine whether or not that organization chart actually works.

It's not that there is one right organization chart that will work for everyone. Of course structure must be tailored to the unique needs of each organization. Nonetheless, there are fundamental principles that will determine how well your organization chart works.

Ignoring that science is perilous. Leaders may solve one problem and create a number of new problems. Every few years, an organization *du jour* attempts to solve the problems created by past restructurings, setting the organization up for a never-ending, painful, and costly series of disruptions.

This book presents the basics of organizational theory, clear definitions of the building blocks of structure, practical principles for combining them into organization charts, and an approach to high-performance teamwork that is far more flexible and powerful than traditional work-flow engineering.

While this overview is no substitute for the over 700-page study from which it was abstracted, its purpose is to introduce leaders to concepts that will help them create the kind of organizations people want to work for, the kind of companies customers want to do business with, and the kind of work environments that engage every bright mind and help everyone succeed.

This book is organized into the following parts:

* Basic theory: the reasons organizations exist, and the fundamental trade-off of structural design.

* Lessons learned: common mistakes and structures that fail. Why repeat the mistakes of the past?

* Building blocks: the basic lines of business that exist within any structure, be it a corporation or an internal-support department.

* Putting the pieces together: simple guidelines for combining the building blocks into a healthy organization chart.

* High-performance teamwork: how to induce fluid, cross-boundary work flows so that the organization chart actually works.

* Ideas to action: How to implement a world-class restructuring; and the traits of an effective leader of structural change.

BASIC THEORY

1. What Is an Organization?

Let's begin this exploration of organizational structure with a definition of the word "organization."

The term "organization" refers to any group of people working together to achieve a common and ongoing purpose — one which benefits people outside their group. It may be a corporation or a company, a government agency, a family working on their farm, a volunteer association, or a union. The organization may seek to make a profit, or it may be not-for-profit.

An organization is different than a project team. Organizations are permanent, or at least intended to survive beyond a single project.

A project team, on the other hand, is a temporary association of people who belong to different parts of an organization (or more than one organization) and agree to work together to achieve a specific deliverable. The project team disbands at the end of the project, while its members continue to work for their respective organizations.

Organizations exist within organizations. The scope of the organization is a matter of your perspective. If you are the CEO of a multinational corporation, your scope may include numerous autonomous companies as well as internal-support departments. If you are the president of a company within that conglomerate, the relevant organization is your company. If you are an executive in charge of a support function within that company, the organization you care most about is your department.

Regardless of your level, your organization can be viewed as a "business within a business." As such, it probably has most of the elements found in any business as a whole: manufacturing of both products and services, customer service and training, a diversity of types of engineers or designers, the need for an integrated product line, and sales and marketing (client liaison) functions.

Organizations exist to serve "markets" — groups of clients who benefit from their activities. If the organization is a company, the market is made up of its customers who are external to the company. If the organization is a department within a company, its market is, for the most part, the rest of the company.

And when viewed as a business within a business, every organization no doubt has intense competition.

When speaking about a company in a competitive free market, this is obvious. But the same is true of support functions within corporations. Internal service providers compete with both outsourcing vendors and decentralization. Even if it seems as though the rest of the company *must* work through your department, the surest way to lose a monopoly is to behave as a monopolist.

Every organization must earn the right to do business with its customers, be they external or internal.

The challenge every executive faces is to build the kind of organization that earns market share through performance, as the vendor of choice in a market that has the right to go elsewhere.

2. Why Organizations Exist

To unravel the science of organizational structure, consider the following question:

Why do organizations exist?

Put another way, why would an organization perform any better than an equal number of individuals, all acting independently?

One obvious answer is that the people within the organization work toward a common purpose. But is common purpose enough?

Picture a number of people who are not part of an organization, but who agree to work toward a common purpose (perhaps by sharing a strategic plan). For example, imagine thousands of individuals agreeing to work independently to make cars. Would you really expect them to compete with Toyota? Or even a small firm such as Morgan?

Getting a number of people to agree to work toward a common purpose solves the problem of quantity, but not of complexity. For very simple tasks, it may be enough. For example, 100 people agreeing to pick up garbage along a stretch of roadside may perform nearly as well as an organization of 100 members. This is because each individual is fully capable of picking up garbage; more than one person is needed only to handle the necessary volume.

We all know that one person cannot do everything. One person cannot make an entire car. To make a car alone, one person would have to be an expert at virtually every branch of design, engineering, procurement, manufacturing, distribution, finance, sales, etc. No individual can possibly know enough about all of these things.

And a collection of individuals with a common purpose cannot perform much better than completely unrelated individuals. Just agreeing on a common purpose is not enough. Even if everyone agreed on the common goal, each individual would still have to design, manufacture, and sell the company's products (as well as arrange for financial resources and build the necessary computer systems) all on their own.

There is a scientific way to explain this obvious truth — a concept that will help explain the reason organizations exist and identify some of the key drivers of organizational performance.

Cybernetics, i.e., systems science, is the study of the control of complex, dynamic systems. A simple example is the thermostat in your home that turns on the heater when it gets too cold and the air conditioner when it gets too hot.

Organizations can be viewed as very large, complex cybernetic systems.

In the science of cybernetics, the term "variety" is defined as the range of possible states of the system at any point in time. It is the complexity inherent in the many disciplines and day-to-day activities of the organization, multiplied by the pace of that activity (i.e., volume of activity per day):

$$VARIETY \ = \ COMPLEXITY \ x \ PACE$$

Variety is a measure of the throughput, or bandwidth, of an individual or organization — one's ability to process information and perform activities in a given period of time.

Each individual is limited in his or her capacity to handle variety. A person can only think so many thoughts in a day, read so much, and know so much; that is, he or she can only process so much variety. For example, an executive cannot know every decision made by each employee each day, since one executive cannot process as much variety as the many people within the organization.

An organization is confronted with tremendous variety. Think of all the knowledge within any one profession, and all the news of emerging techniques and technologies that a professional must keep up with. Then, multiply that complexity by all the many disciplines involved in making a car. Finally, multiply all that by the pace of events around that globe that affect a car manufacturer's business. This level of variety is unthinkable for any one individual.

It's a fundamental truth that people are limited in their variety-processing abilities. The question is, what can one do with a finite capacity for variety?

People can use their finite variety-processing ability to know a little bit about everything — the generalist who is a "jack of all trades and master of none." But then they would never know enough about any one field to master it, and certainly not enough to build a car.

The truth is, *people can only be world-class experts at one thing at a time.* We may rotate among specialties in the course of our careers. But at any point in time, each of us must concentrate on a well-defined area of expertise to remain competitive.

Specialists use their variety-processing abilities to learn one profession in depth. Of course, in order to work with others, specialists must use a little bit of their variety-processing abilities to know a little about everything else. With that caveat, by focusing on one field of study, specialists become very good at one thing.

Then, when specialists cooperate with each other by forming an organization, the organization has both depth and breadth.

Organizations perform better than individuals only to the extent that they permit specialization. Said another way, organizations exist specifically to allow people to specialize. Within some practical limits, *the more that people specialize, the more depth they achieve and the better the organization can perform.*

But wait! There's a catch....

3. The Catch

Imagine an organization made of specialists, all of whom are very good at their respective professions, but each of whom acts independently without coordination. How well would this organization perform?

Terribly! Actually, it would do worse than a collection of independent generalists. Since no one specialist sees the big picture, collectively they would be unlikely to get any products out the door.

Here's the catch: The more people specialize, the more they become interdependent. Put simply, *specialization depends on teamwork.*

If people within an organization are not good at forming teams across organizational boundaries, then they cannot afford to specialize. Each small group must replicate all the skills it's likely to need to avoid dependence on others. This is sometimes called the "stovepipe" organization, since it is made up of a set of self-sufficient groups of generalists that do not work well together — like a bunch of vertical pipes that never touch.

Of course, stovepipe organizations forgo the advantages of their size and perform no better than a number of small companies. They might as well be broken up by a leveraged buy-out (or in the case of a staff function, decentralized).

Conversely, the better the organization is at teamwork, the more it can afford to specialize. Indeed, *the gating factor in many organizations is not money or people, but the mechanisms that coordinate people on teams.*

Teamwork among specialists, then, is essential to organizational performance — in fact, to the very existence of organizations.

Therefore, coordinating mechanisms (processes that build teamwork) are as important as the organization chart in building healthy, high-performance organizations.

For this reason, any approach to organizational structure must address both the division of labor (the organization chart which determines people's specialties) and the coordinating mechanisms (which define work flows and combine people from throughout the organization on project teams to accomplish an organization's various objectives).

Some people believe that organizations should be structured so as to reduce the need for teamwork, to "minimize hand-offs." They accept as a given the current teaming capabilities of the organization, and design the structure around that constraint.

This book takes a different approach. To borrow a phrase from the Olympics, it "goes for the gold." It discusses how to optimize the organization chart, and then how to build the necessary level of teamwork required to make that organization of interdependent specialists work.

In summary, **organizations exist in order to allow people to** *specialize*...

   which in turn depends on excellence at *teamwork*.

Therefore, to design a healthy structure, one must simultaneously design the organization chart and the coordinating processes that make teams work.

LESSONS LEARNED

4. Healthy Organizations

In this section, we'll examine a number of common mistakes and structures that fail. But first, let's envision a standard of excellence — what we'll call a "healthy" organization.

It is easy to spot a healthy organization. Consider some of the traits of a well-designed organizational structure:

*   Everybody is clearly focused on excellence in their specialty. Ask anybody in the organization, and they'll be able to tell you what business they're in and what they're supposed to be excellent at. People naturally develop their competencies, keep up with their professions, and take pride in their work.

*   There are no impossible jobs. Jobs are not designed to require people to be experts at too many things at once; i.e., designed for "super-people." Instead, jobs are designed such that most people can succeed, and super-people can super-achieve.

*   People are not in competition with their peers, since territories don't overlap.

*   People of like professions are clustered together, so that they naturally swap tricks of the trade and produce integrated, not fragmented, results.

*   No group is in business to put another group out of business; i.e., adversarial relations are not designed into the organization chart.

*   No group is in a dead-end business without a future. Everybody has both current responsibilities, and opportunities for career growth.

*   All needed lines of business (now and into the future) are covered by some group. Domains (job descriptions) are written in such as way as both to clearly specify where

everything goes today, and to determine who's responsible for discovering new things in the future.

*   Nobody is put in a conflict-of-interests situation where succeeding at one of their missions (e.g., keeping operations running) undermines another of their missions (e.g., inventing the next generation).

*   Jobs are "whole" — designed around lines of business rather than tasks on an assembly line. People feel ownership of their "business within a business," and do everything it takes to keep their piece of the business competitive and to please their customers. Jobs are rich, interesting, fulfilling, and motivational. Entrepreneurship blasts away bureaucracy.

*   Accountabilities are clear, and people are empowered with all the authority they need to run their business with a minimum of impediments from bureaucracy and peer groups. In every case, everywhere, authority matches accountabilities.

*   People have a clear understanding of their product lines and their customers within the organization. People accept responsibility for results, rather than "punching the clock" or "going through the motions." A best-effort mentality is replaced with a focus on results.

*   Project (and service) teams form fluidly across structural boundaries because anyone has the right to "buy" help from peer groups. Internal subcontracting gathers just the right resources at just the right time on every team, with clear individual accountability and a clear chain of command. In other words, everyone is a "process owner" who flexibly arranges help from the prior stage in order to satisfy the next stage of the process.

Healthy organizations can be relatively flat, that is, with wide spans of control rather than with excessive layers of supervision. This works because people are, to a greater extent, self managing. They have clearly defined lines of business, and take responsibility for running their businesses within the business as independent, empowered entrepreneurs.

People are also interdependent. They team without management intervention, getting whatever help they need directly from peers.

And they're relatively free of the unpleasant politics that come from internal competition.

In short, a healthy organization engages everybody and empowers them to contribute all they can, and it doesn't waste any energy on anything other than serving internal customers and achieving the strategic objectives of the firm.

You really don't need to read the rest of this book if your organization meets all these criteria.

5. Symptoms of an Unhealthy Organizational Structure

Still reading? If you have concerns about your organization's structure, be assured that you're not alone.

Unfortunately, the symptoms of a poorly designed organization are all too familiar. But they're not always recognized as structural problems.

Despite an ever growing body of evidence, some still believe that formal structure has little real impact on these problems. In their view, success depends on great people, motivated by a culture of teamwork, who altruistically think beyond their job descriptions and do what's right.

Sure, it's possible for superior people motivated by an excellent leader and a spirit of teamwork to overcome structural dys-functions. However, to do so, managers will have to waste their precious time dealing with the friction created by structural problems. And this is a fragile truce; a change in the composition or character of the leadership team could fracture the camaraderie and disable the organization.

A brief story illustrates the powerful impact of organizational structure on people's performance.

A large airline divided its IS department into two computer centers: conventional IS, and its reservations system. Reporting to each computer-center director was a systems-engineering manager.

On the conventional IS side, top management became very frustrated because the department retained an archaic mainframe. The systems-engineering manager had failed to implement a new platform, so they fired him for lack of technological innovation.

Two years later, they fired the next systems-engineering manager for the same reason.

Two years after that, still another manager was fired.

These systems-engineering managers were all bright, seasoned people who were good at their professions. The problem wasn't their lack of ability.

Put yourself in the shoes of this systems-engineering manager. Your boss is the computer-center director. He is paid to keep things running *reliably, safely, and cheaply.* Would you dare suggest a new mainframe? Of course not!

Your boss, head of computer operations, is rewarded for stability; and the implementation of a new platform (a significant change) inevitably disrupts operational stability. Since the boss is paid to resist change, the manager of systems engineering tasked with change is destined to fail.

This clearly is a structural problem. If a change function reports to an operational function, little progress will occur — no matter who has the job of change. It is both futile and cruel to blame the systems-engineering manager for poor performance when the fault lies in the organizational structure.

Unhealthy organizational structures build conflicts into the work environment, and they burn people out. They create untenable jobs, fail to align people's efforts with business strategies, and cause people to waste significant time resolving internal political issues.

The above case study illustrates one symptom of a poorly designed structure: a lack of innovation.

Consider a few more problems — troublesome from the viewpoint of both staff and clients — whose root cause can be traced to the organization's structure:

* **Lack of strategic partnership with clients:** "Clients don't understand the strategic potential of our products, and don't invite us to participate in their planning processes. We are a passive utility that is here to deliver only what is asked of us."

   The structure may be missing a sales and marketing (client liaison) function.

* **Clients unwilling to be open with the organization:** "Our clients treat us as outsiders rather than part of their management teams. They mistrust us and are reluctant to share information."

   The structure may define staff's jobs as controlling clients rather than serving them, or it may instruct people to look after excellence in their technologies and disciplines (sell only Rolls-Royces) rather than take care of customers with appropriate solutions.

* **Pressure for decentralizaton or outsourcing:** "Our clients would rather do it themselves or hire our competitors than do business with us."

   Again, the lack of a client liaison function may be the root cause. Or staff may not view their jobs as running businesses within the business and view clients as customers; instead, they may feel that their job is to do whatever they think is best for the company.

* **Slow pace of innovation:** "All my job allows me to do is crank out day-to-day work. I don't have the time (or permission) to explore new developments in my profession."

   Some structures only define accountability for traditional

products and have not identified who's to study the many emerging product lines.

Even worse, structure may put people in a conflict-of-interests situation, being held responsible for both operational stability and innovation.

* **Fragmentation, and lack of integration:** "My job is to build good solutions, and standards only get in the way." Alternatively, "My project should determine the future architecture for the entire market (company)."

When structure is missing a key element such as a standards coordinator, a reliable process of consensus building on standards and policies is unlikely, and fragmentation results.

* **Confused accountabilities, territorial disputes, empire building, and other management headaches:** "I spend so much of my time in meetings resolving internal disputes and making sure the organization works that I hardly have time to do my job or think strategically."

Success may be measured by the size of your empire rather than competitive advantage, customer satisfaction, and market share. This is common when people don't understand that their jobs are running businesses within the business.

* **Lack of teamwork:** "That's your job, not mine. I'm not going to divert my efforts and take personal risk to help you."

Boundaries may not be clear and distinct, and jobs may not be defined as serving internal customers.

* **Demotivated people, or an anti-management sentiment:** "There's no way for me to have much impact on this organization, or to get ahead in this company. I'm just putting in my time."

Structure may define jobs in terms of tasks and responsibilities, rather than lines of business.   In such cases, structure does not permit empowerment or entrepreneurship.

Each of these problems may be traced directly to the organizational structure (in whole or in part).   It would do little good to address the symptoms with cultural values, strategic plans, or new technologies.   And it certainly doesn't do any good to blame people who respond to organizational influences and do exactly what they are paid to do.   If the structure is dysfunctional, a brilliant vision, top-notch people, and plentiful resources will still produce disappointing results.   The only effective answer is restructuring.

Certainly not all performance problems are structural, but organizational structure is one of the most critical determinants of performance.   The power of organizational structure must not be underestimated.

Good people in a poor organizational structure will fail, while average people in a healthy structure can succeed.

Organizational structure should be high on the agenda of any leader who intends to build a high-performance organization.

6. Why Study Mistakes?

So many organizations suffer the symptoms of poor structure described in Chapter 5, wasting time and money and constraining effectiveness (sometimes to the point of risking extinction).

Why would leaders tolerate this?

In many cases, it just happened. Most organizational structures have evolved over many years under a number of different executives, each with his or her own philosophy about organizational structure. Adjustments were made to accommodate new technologies and services, special projects, and occasionally to handle individual career issues. Periodically, job descriptions and working relationships were revised as cyclic pressures for centralization and decentralization were felt.

The resulting organizational structures seemed reasonable at the time; but in the cold light of objective analysis, they may, in fact, be haphazard and dysfunctional.

There is another factor to consider. As described in Chapter 2, the purpose of an organization is to process more variety than individuals alone can handle. But most organizations evolved in a much simpler, lower-variety period of time.

Now, the variety surrounding them is exploding; and organizations are not equiped to handle it. In other words, structures that may have worked adequately in a simpler time may now be bursting at the seams.

Consider the many sources of variety that organizations must now deal with:

*   Clients are more educated and more demanding.

*   Technological complexity is exploding at an accelerating pace.

* Economic volatility is frightening.

* Geo-political shifts are often unforeseeable.

* Current events anywhere in the world can affect your markets.

* Increasingly complex legal and regulatory restrictions are bewildering.

* Potential competitors or partners can be anywhere in the world.

* Organizations are getting larger and more complex.

These changes in the business environment are matched by an accelerated pace of change in virtually every function and profession.

If the only problem were the need for increased speed and flexibility, an effective response might be to break the organization up into small, autonomous business units. However, doing so reduces the degree of specialization, making the organization less capable of dealing with complexity.

If the only problem were increased complexity, an organization might partition itself into highly focused groups of specialists and expand the management hierarchy to coordinate them. But this is expensive, and can jeopardize the organization's ability to get work done quickly and flexibly.

If the only problem were cost, an organization might eliminate layers of management and simplify its processes. But as the management hierarchy is reduced, so are the coordinating mechanisms. The organization becomes less able to adapt to a changing environment with flexible, cross-functional work processes. And as processes are simplified, the organization becomes more rigid (like an assembly line) and less capable of dealing with rapidly changing business demands.

The real problem is the combination of the need for speed and flexibility, specialization (to handle complexity), and efficiency and cost effectiveness. These factors add up to (actually, they *multiply* to) an explosion in variety that is taxing the limits of today's organizations.

There are some popular short-cuts....

Some say an organization must choose whether it will focus on customer intimacy, technical excellence, or operational efficiency. In fact, there is no reason why an organization cannot be world-class at all of these things. But to do so, it will have to learn to handle much more variety.

Some are quite willing to sacrifice their staff by demanding unreasonable efforts — inducing high turnover, animosities, ulcers, or worse — to succeed in spite of their bad organizational designs.

Some are even willing to sacrifice their ethics to get the job done in spite of their self-imposed hurdles.

We should be grateful to those executives who have, in the past, taken these shortcuts. They've taught us what *not* to do.

In the rest of this section, we'll examine some structural approaches that have failed. The goal of this section is to help you avoid repeating the mistakes of the past, and to illustrate some principles of organizational design that will be applied to constructing healthy organizations.

7. Internal Competition

Some leaders think that putting their subordinates in competition with one another will hone their skills and elicit the best performance from everyone. They might also argue that it maximizes creativity, with different alternatives coming from the various competing groups.

Internal competition is created consciously when two groups are given overlapping territories. It's created inadvertently when boundaries are unclear. In either case, the effect is the same: staff are paid to compete with one another.

In fact, artificial internal competition should never be needed.

In any line of business, be it producing the company's products or providing internal support services, there's plenty of real competition in the form of outsourcing. Nothing is sacred. Product development, manufacturing, sales, and all the support functions can be — and have been — turned over to external "business partners."

Even an apparent monopoly — where a group is designated the only internal supplier of a given product or service — doesn't protect staff from external competition. All that a monopoly does is make the market-share equation zero or one. If internal customers become disgruntled, they don't begin to drift away (providing an early warning that change is needed). Instead, they're forced to wait until things get so bad and pressures build to the point where the whole function is outsourced.

Another very real source of competition is decentralization. Whenever an internal customer chooses to make your products and services for themselves rather than buy from your group, you've lost market share. Certainly when divisions set up support functions in parallel with corporate staff, the notion of losing business to competition (albeit friendly competition) should be obvious.

With no shortage of real competitors, staff *must* offer the best deal to remain in business. If they don't know this fundamental truth — that is, if they don't recognize that they face competition — it's not too tough for leaders to point out the obvious.

And if staff still don't believe they have competition, an outsourcing or benchmarking study can serve as a wake-up call and provide motivational metrics of staff's competitiveness (even if leaders don't attempt to give away a precious asset).

The truth is, you don't need to use structure to get staff to understand that they're in business to please internal customers, and that they have to earn customers' business through performance to keep their jobs.

Meanwhile, the costs of pitting staff against one another are high.

When more than one group maintains the same expertise, does the same kinds of research, and produces the same types of products, precious resources are wasted. This drives costs up.

More insidiously, when two groups share the same domain, each cannot specialize as much as if they had different areas of focus. (Consider two competing "engineering" groups, each trying to do everything, as compared with one "product engineering" and one "manufacturing engineering" group.)

When specialization is reduced, people don't accumulate as much experience or offer as much depth of knowledge on any given topic. Since they're less proficient, costs rise and quality suffers.

Furthermore, generalists can't keep up with the literature as well as specialists can, so the pace of innovation slows.

And since they're more likely to be at the bottom of the learning curve, time to market slows.

Another obvious effect of internal competition is that it undermines teamwork. Even if it's a friendly competition, even if it's limited to just part of their work, when people are paid to fight with one another, they generally won't collaborate. No amount of team-building exercises, top-management exhortations, or defined business processes can overcome this fundamental force built into the structure.

A side-effect of unclear boundaries (one cause of internal competition) is that people don't know what they're supposed to be good at. As a result, everybody follows their personal interests, and overlaps and gaps in knowledge occur. If fuzzy boundaries cause gaps as well as internal competition, the organization will miss opportunities; and with no one covering the territory, it won't even know what it missed.

Whether it's consciously pitting people against one another or inadvertently leaving boundaries vague, internal competition doesn't work. Every group needs a clearly defined and discrete domain.

8. Stovepipes

Another popular theory of structure is the "autonomous business unit."

It's argued that, to hold someone accountable for a line of business, you've got to give him or her authority over all the needed factors of production. So far, so good. But some leaders go on to say that this entails putting all the needed support functions structurally under them. In other words, they believe that the only way to give a business-unit leader control is to give him or her the headcount.

A similar argument is put forward within internal service departments. Some say that, to hold a manager accountable for a set of products or services, you've got to give him or her all the various support functions needed to do the job.

Indeed, this was the stated goal of the then-popular "business process reengineering" fad of the 1990's. A self-sufficient organization was built for each of the major business processes, each with all the skills needed in the process.

The result is a "stovepipe" organization where each group is self-sufficient. In other words, each support function or skill is scattered among the various internal-customer groups that need it.

This approach has three major costs: it fragments a function; it creates conflicts of interests; and it damages careers.

First, *fragmenting a function:*   When a function that everybody needs is scattered among the various stovepipes, each little pocket of the function must cover the entire profession as generalists. Conversely, if they were all in one group, the professionals in that function could specialize to a much greater degree.

Generalists produce the familiar results of higher costs, lower quality, reduced pace of innovation, and slower time to market.

Scattering the "campus" of similar experts also reduces the ability of the people in the function to swap lessons learned, tricks of the trade, and professional discoveries. This serves to further reduce quality and increase costs.

As an example, consider the manufacturing function in a global heavy-equipment products company. In the spirit of autonomy, each business unit built its own manufacturing plants. As a result, economies of scale were lost. Capacity sat idle in one plant while another was pressured beyond its capacity; ultimately, lots of excess capacity was built into the system.

One division had a plant in a country while another division did not; instead of using the local capacity, the other division shipped its products in from its plant in a neighboring country, and transportation costs rose.

One division pioneered new manufacturing techniques, but other divisions didn't learn about them until much later when the CEO intervened and commissioned a corporatewide task-force to rationalize production capacity.

And while there could have been significant economies if some plants were designed around long, stable manufacturing runs while others were designed for rapid re-tooling, none of the divisions alone could afford to specialize to that degree.

This same company provided another example of stovepipes: Each division had its own design engineering function. As you might expect, the number of parts the corporation had to buy or make skyrocketed. Another CEO-chartered task force found a dozen different electric motors with roughly the same specifications.

The name of the function doesn't matter — in information technology, a dozen different general-ledger systems; in human resources, a dozen different compensation plans. There's no way around it. Fragmenting a function reduces specialization and discards synergies.

Second, *conflicts of interests:* When a leader is given managerial responsibility for a variety of functions — everything needed to do the job — he or she must manage functions that have conflicting objectives.

For example, some functions keep things running (maintain stability). Others invent new things (shake things up). When one person manages both, a conflict of interests occurs. (Recall the airline's IS department discussed in Chapter 5.) Generally, fire-fighting swamps innovation, short-term interests swamp long-term, and the pace of innovation suffers.

Another common example of a conflict of interests arises when product management is combined with sales. Each product division may be given its own sales force. Or in internal service departments, each specialty within a support function may be responsible for it own internal client relations.

As a result, the customer faces multiple points of contact; i.e., multiple "account representatives" call on each customer. This has a number of serious costs:

For one, customers are unlikely to invite the organization into their strategic planning (a goal in any customer partnership). They have to develop their strategies to the point of knowing what they need to buy before knowing which account representative to call. So much for getting in the door early!

Furthermore, with multiple account representatives calling on every customer, each representative has to call on a greater number of accounts and has less time to spend with any one. As a result, account representatives get to know their customers less well, and the partnership is further distanced.

But the worst effect is the conflict of interests this creates. Account representatives are supposed to be business driven, and help customers translate their business strategies into the right mix of the organization's products and services.

But each account representative sells a subset of the product line. Instead of helping clients diagnose their business needs in a strategy-driven manner, they become product-driven "solutions in search of a problem." Clients learn not to trust them, or at least to hold them at arm's length. Again, partnership is undermined.

In short, giving each division its own sales force (or expecting each internal support group to do its own client-liaison work) undermines the very purpose of a sales force.

Third, *damaged careers:* It's pretty tough for the executive at the head of a stovepipe organization to be good at managing people in a diversity of disciplines. Generally, mentoring is weak and careers suffer in all but the primary profession of the executive.

Furthermore, career paths are destroyed when a profession is embedded in its customer organizations. In these small, scattered pockets of the profession, when it comes to career advancement, there's no place to go.

Holding people accountable for results is a good thing. And it's true that you can't hold people accountable if you don't give them authority over the resources they need to do the job.

But you don't need to build stovepipe structures to match authority to accountability. Doing so is like saying that to control what you eat, you need to own your own grocery store!

The truth is, you can give leaders full authority over all the functions they need as *customers* rather than bosses.

The real problem stems from the belief that people won't serve you well if they don't report to you. However, when businesses within a business recognize their internal customers and work to please them, leaders can get all the support they need without having to move the headcount under them (just as in the real world when we buy help from our suppliers).

9. Customer-aligned Structures

The customer-aligned structure is now common in a wide variety of internal support functions.

Internal support functions include traditional service organizations like finance, human resources, administration, and information technology. They also include functions like engineering, manufacturing, and sales that are in a position to help various product managers throughout a company.

In all such functions, people are coming to recognize the need for customer focus — an organization tuned to please its internal customers. The function must understand its customers and their business strategies, and build close partnerships by providing consistent points of contact.

It must also give customers the power to set priorities within their finite shares of the organization's resources.

In an attempt to be customer focused, some organizations have aligned their structures with the customers' organization chart. They divide their profession by customer organization. In other words, each customer gets a little group of generalists dedicated to their needs.

Some companies even go so far as to move the client-structured groups to report to client business units, i.e., decentralization.

This customer-aligned structure is similar to the stovepipe structure. Like the stovepipe organization, it scatters each profession among the various customer-centered groups.

All the same dysfunctions result: generalists are more costly than specialists, produce lower quality, lag in innovation, and are slower to market with new ideas. Meanwhile, reinvention, inconsistent directions, and fragmented results are to be expected.

Furthermore, this is a slippery slope to decentralization. In fact, the organization might as well be broken up, since it is not taking advantage of the synergies of being one integrated organization. [1]

Some have attempted to ameliorate some of the problems with a "matrix" structure. In this structure, everyone has two bosses: one responsible for the profession, and the other representing the customers. The boss responsible for the profession is supposed to ensure consistent methods, facilitate the sharing of lessons learned, and provide viable career paths. The customer boss sets priorities and directs work.

In practice, the matrix has not worked well. Customers still own a small group of generalists, instead of having access to any of the many specialists in an integrated function. And by now, you know all the problems that result from generalists instead of specialists.

If the staff in a matrixed group do specialize, other problems arise. Customers get only those products or services which the specialists in their little groups know.

Even if a customer's latest project requires a different mix of skills, customers have difficulty getting help from the right specialists; those people are dedicated to other customers, and the organization cannot be restructured whenever a new project begins.

As a result of this inflexibility, projects are not always staffed with the people best qualified to do them.

Dedicating groups to customers is an attempt to solve three problems: getting staff to be customer focused, building a deep understanding of customers' businesses, and giving customers control over priorities.

---

1.   For more on decentralization, see: Meyer, N. Dean. *Decentralization: Fantasies, Failings, and Fundamentals.*

These three problems are not rooted in structure, and can be more effectively addressed in other ways.

Customer focus is a matter of culture — the habits and practices within the organization — and can be addressed by teaching staff the specific behaviors that embody the spirit of customer focus.

Knowing the customers and their businesses is the job of account representatives. If the organization includes an effective client-liaison function, there's no need to dedicate entire groups of product designers and service-delivery functions to each customer.

Control over priorities is a function of the resource-management processes in the organization, what we term the "internal economy." Customers can be given spending power rather than dedicated staff, either through a fee-for-service economy (chargebacks) or (perhaps more practically) through a process that lets customers decide how to spend the finite hours that staff have available. 2

Structure is not a "silver bullet" that can solve every problem. When problems rooted in other organizational systems are addressed through structure, they're rarely addressed well and many other problems are created.

Customer-aligned structures may succeed at enhancing short-term customer satisfaction; but in the long run, they cause more problems than they solve.

2.   For more on the internal economy, see: Meyer, N. Dean. *The Internal Economy* (forthcoming).

10. New Versus Old

You really need to get a major new project out the door. It's huge, and requires a mix of skills from throughout your organization. You're worried that if you give responsibility for this major endeavor to one of your existing managers, it'll get lost in the shuffle of day-to-day priorities.

From the other perspective, since this project is so important, you're worried that the responsible manager may only focus on the "hot" project and neglect other less glamorous, but still essential, maintenance work.

You're also privately worried that your organization isn't good enough at teamwork to staff such a big, complex project on an ad hoc basis.

So you create a new box on your organization chart for this project, and staff it with a young, up-and-coming manager. Under this manager, you assign people with the needed skills, moving their positions from their past managers to this new project manager.

In other words, you create two kinds of groups:

> one doing the new project, the remainder maintaining the old product base;

>> one building the future, the rest maintaining "legacy" products and services;

>>> one politically visible with tremendous career opportunities, the remainder a career dead-end with all the fun, new work taken away from them;

>>>> one group in business to put the rest out of business.

Inadvertantly, you create two classes of citizenship, and build rivalry into the organization.

The facts are the same whenever an "emerging technologies" function is embodied in the organization chart, a group whose job is to discover the new opportunities in everybody else's lines of business.

This structure is intended to balance resources among various needs: supporting past products, delivering the new project, and developing the next generation of products beyond that.

Fencing off resources for various purposes occurs naturally in an effective internal economy. But using structure to solve resource-management problems has a number of unintended consequences:

Both the new and the old groups need to cover the same intellectual ground. The organization needs two of every profession. This reduces the degree of specialization.

Meanwhile, all learning about the future is concentrated in one small group. This takes away from everyone else the responsibility for thinking about the future, and undermines their entrepreneurial spirit. It also creates a bottleneck for learning that actually slows the pace of innovation in the organization. In other words, it wastes bright minds throughout the organization, and limits learning to a few (rather than many) bright minds.

The rivalries that inevitably result constrain teamwork. There is a tremendous amount of business knowledge embedded in the current products and the groups that support them. This may not be well utilized in the design of the new project.

Furthermore, there's little incentive to do things right the first time. The new group can get the glory by getting the project out quickly, and leave to the old group which inherits their work the task of fixing their errors. Without first-time quality, costs rise.

To make quality matters worse, clients are faced with a choice: wait for the right answer in the new project, or get it done now the old way. Competition for clients' business may induce staff to offer "quick and dirty" solutions that may be difficult to maintain.

The two "classes of citizenship" also lead to morale problems. People in the new group tend to become arrogant. Meanwhile, they spend a lot of time worrying about their next job, and may prolong projects unnecessarily to maintain their employment and their privileged position.

The old groups feel demoralized — rightly so if they find themselves in dead-end jobs. This leads to job dissatisfaction, low productivity, and high turnover.

Of course, this approach to new projects is not scalable. Over time, the organization would have to be restructured whenever major projects begin and end.

And your private concern, the organization's ability to form project teams across structural boundaries, is never really addressed. Thus, smaller projects may still lack the cross-boundary teamwork that they need to succeed.

In a healthy organization, every group both delivers its current products and develops the new products that will obsolete their current work. In a healthy organization, everybody has a future.

And reserving time for new projects, for maintaining existing products, and for anything else is left to the organization's resource-management processes.

Again, the lesson is: Don't solve with structure a problem rooted in your internal economy.

11. Means Versus Ends

In some cases, leaders know that they should divide up the organization chart in a way that gives each group its own unique specialty. But trouble can occur if groups are divided by *means rather than ends,* the wrong choice of specialty.

For example, engineers (developers) might be divided by the platforms they build on, or by the tools and languages they use, rather than by what they build.

Choosing the wrong specialty fragments a profession, resulting in many of the problems described in prior chapters.

As in Chapter 7, internal competition occurs whenever two different means (platforms, tools, languages) can be used to produce the same end result (a product or service). Two groups compete for the job, instead of a single group offering two alternatives.

The worst manifestations of this is new versus old means, as discussed in Chapter 10.

As in the stovepipes described in Chapter 8, multiple groups must replicate the same expertise: knowledge of the products themselves. Thus, specialization in their most critical expertise is reduced.

Structuring by means instead of ends also introduces unwelcome biases. Groups will produce products by the current methods, processes, and tools rather than seek the most appropriate means for the project at hand. Creativity and innovation are lost, and barriers to progress are institutionalized when people cling to old ways in order to maintain their jobs.

And whose job is it to discover new methods, tools, and processes — new means to the same ends? We're forced back to the "emerging technologies" group that causes so much trouble, as described in in Chapter 10.

Organizations must learn to engage everyone in improving the organization every day, in the course of doing their daily jobs. This can only be accomplished through a powerful principle: *empowerment.*

Empowerment is based on matching authority and accountability. Whenever one group has authority and another has accountability, serious problems result. The controller, having authority without accountability, inevitably becomes a tyrant. The controlled, having accountability without authority, becomes a scapegoat and a victim.

People are empowered when they're given all the information, resources, and decision-making power they need to accomplish their assigned deliverables.

A critical aspect of empowerment is managing people by results, not by how they accomplish them. Put simply, people should be given jobs to do and left free (and supported) to discover the best means (tasks, methods, tools, and processes) to accomplish them.

Fundamental to this principle, structure should divide groups by the *products and services they produce,* not the ways they go about making them.

In this light, a structure is suspect if it leaves groups without clear and distinct product lines, or if it divides a single product line among groups. Three other examples of this are:

*   *Pools* of project managers or professionals who are called upon to deliver other groups' products and services.

This puts the burden on generalists to produce products and services in everyone else's specialty. And note that these people are leading critical projects, but they don't have a long-term commitment to the group's particular product line.

Meanwhile, this structure relieves everyone else of account-ability for their own product lines.

Furthermore, it creates an atmosphere of two classes of

citizenship. Either people in the pool are considered heroes who rescue everyone else when the going gets tough, or they're nothing more than "warm bodies" who do as they're told.

*   *Division by tasks* rather than products, i.e., by what people do rather than what they produce. A common example is a group whose job is to plan another group's business, or do research on another's products. Another example is a group that does the first few steps in producing a product and another group that finishes the job, dividing the structure by steps on an assembly line.

    In this structure, no one feels accountable for the end results — the products of the organization.

    No one is responsible for improving the overall process. Instead, each group sub-optimizes (and perpetuates) their steps in the current process.

    And no one is responsible for discovering future products or planning the strategy for this business within a business.

*   A *quality control* function where inspectors are responsible for catching others' mistakes, relieving everyone else of responsibility for their own quality.

    This leads to lower quality since those doing the work feel free to make more mistakes, and to higher costs due to the need for rework.

    Whenever one group is in business to control another group, neither is empowered to run the business. This violates the basic principle of matching authority and accountability.

Designing a healthy, empowered structure is a matter of dividing the organization's various internal and external products and services among its groups. This gives everybody whole jobs, and every group is assured of its own business within a business.

12. Missing Functions

The last chapter concluded with the vision of a structure where groups are delineated by their products and services. To do this requires knowledge of the entire range of products and services produced by the organization, including all those sold internally as well as those sold to clients.

If any are forgotten, those functions will not happen with world-class excellence or with reliability.

For example, in any internal support function, there's the job of account representative — the client liaison who builds partnerships with the corporation's business units, and links clients' strategic needs to the organization's product line.

Too often, this critical function is left to senior managers, as time permits. None have enough time to spend with clients, or to perfect the methods of strategic needs assessment.

Furthermore, senior managers have biases originating from the specific product lines their groups represent, so they do a poor job of offering unbiased business advice. As a result, strategic opportunities are lost and partnerships suffer.

This is one, albeit common, example of a missing function. Similarly, if any product, technology, or service function is missing, the organization will someday find itself with a gap in its product line.

Designing an effective structure requires a framework that defines every line of business in an entire organization. (Such a framework is described in the next section of this book.)

13. Summary: Design Requirements

The problems described in this section show how painful a poorly designed structure can be.

Certainly, the executives who created them had good intentions. And many can point to well-considered reasons that made sense at the time.

Sadly, some can't even do that. They let client pressures dictate their structure, or avoid the real issues like the internal economy or organizational culture. Or they adapt the structure to accommodate personalities or individuals' career interests.

For whatever reasons, the truth is that most restructuring efforts are based on opinions and guesswork rather than science.

Everyone has an opinion about organizational structure, and people have experimented with a tremendous variety of approaches. The problems they intended to address are quite real. But with the many conflicting forces at work, it is all too easy to make subtle mistakes that solve some problems while creating many others.

The response may be yet another organizational experiment. Some executives repeatedly change their organization's structure — one year decentralizing and the next recentralizing; now organizing by technologies and later by client groupings — each restructuring fixing the mistakes of the last while creating its own problems. In some cases, every new product or service requires a new organization. In the worst cases, whenever anything goes wrong, the executive restructures the organization again.

Repeated reorganization is highly disruptive and expensive. This thrashing — the "organization *du jour*" — is a symptom of leaders who lack an understanding of the *science* of organizational structure.

On the other hand, with a scientific approach, leaders can address the diversity of demands in the short term with an approach that provides a consistent evolutionary direction for the long term.

Looking at the problems discussed above, further evidence of the need for a better way, we also see the makings of that science — clear requirements that are the objectives of a systematic design of organization charts.

The requirements demonstrated in these case studies include the following:

* Provide every group with *clear domains.* Make sure every group knows exactly what its territory is.

* Ensure that *all possible product lines are included.* If it's no one's job, it won't happen. Make sure the organization chart is comprehensive, with every possible line of business (whether resourced today or not) covered by some group.

* Ensure no overlaps, i.e., *distinct domains.* Utilize external competition as a source of benchmarks of performance, but never build internal competition by pitting people against their peers.

* *Structure by specialty.* Structure tells people what they're supposed to be good at. Trust teamwork to get people help from other specialties, instead of multi-disciplinary stovepipes. And put all those in the same profession together under a common boss.

* *Distinguish customers from bosses.* Each group should be allowed to serve any customers, anywhere, who wish to buy its unique line of products and services. Only account representatives should be associated with specific customers.

* *Structure to deliver what customers ask of you, not as customers wish you to structure.* Earn customers' business by providing the best products and services at the best price, and by investing in partnership. Use your knowledge of your profession to structure in the way you know best, and leave it

to your internal "account representatives" to link clients to the new structure.

*   *Give every group a future.* If staff don't seem to have time to think about the future, look into your internal economy and solve the resources problem there. But don't fence off resources by creating new structural groups. Give every group responsibility both for delivering current products and services, and for planning and developing its future business within a business.

*   Give people *whole, empowered jobs.* Design structure by dividing the organization's many products and services, sold to clients and one another. Avoid groups defined by tasks, or by how they do their work (processes, methods, tools). Design organization charts as interlocking businesses.

Hopefully, these requirements seem like common sense. They should, because they're based on a fundamental aspect of human nature: People do what you reward them to do.

Structure sends signals that tell people what to do. In a poorly designed structure, people are told to fight with one another, seek independence rather than interdependence, disempower one another, and cling to old ways.

But when done well, by designing the signals systematically, structure can be the basis for empowerment, customer focus, cross-boundary teamwork, entrepreneurship, and competitive edge.

The remainder of this book gives an overview of the science of structural design: the basic building blocks of structure, how to assemble them into an organization chart, and how to build the cross-boundary teamwork needed to make any organization chart work.

BUILDING BLOCKS

14. What Are Building Blocks?

In this section of the book, the fundamental building blocks of structure are defined. These building blocks are found in any organization, be it an entire corporation or a support function in a division.

This framework of building blocks provides a basis for discussions of structure. Too often, leaders get together and plan a new organization chart. But each leaves with a different understanding of what words like "engineering" and "operations" means. The result is an arduous, sometime embarrassing, public adventure in sorting out what the new organization chart really means.

Using this common language, executives can analyze their current structure and lessons learned; understand others' proposals precisely; and make structural decisions in a factual, analytic manner.

This framework can also be used to ensure that every aspect of an organization's mission is assigned, and that people have clear and non-overlapping territories.

By the way, the terms are chosen to be different, perhaps even odd. Familiar terms bring the baggage of past definitions, so vivid in our minds, and so different from the images evoked in others' minds by exactly those same words. If this language of structural design helps but proves uncomfortable, use it in the planning phase and then translate it into more understandable terms when you're ready for public consumption.

I'll warn you in advance: The language is "rigged" in three ways.

1.   Each building block represents a whole job, a line of business rather than a set of tasks or roles.

2.   Each is a distinct profession, important enough to be worthy of profession specialization.

     At the high level, they're too big to be a single profession, but rather comprise many related professions. Drill down within any of the building blocks to the next level of detail, and you'll see professions within professions, each worthy of specialization if the size of the organization permits.

3.   None requires conflicts of interests. Each building block has a unique perspective that contributes to the organization's overall balance of paradoxical objectives.

One caveat before we begin the tour of the building blocks of structure. The building blocks are not, in themselves, an organization chart. They're a language executives can use to design a structure tailored to the unique needs of each organization.

At the highest level, there are five building blocks of structure (see Figure 1):

*   Technologists.
*   Service Bureaus.
*   Coordinators.
*   Consultants.
*   Auditors.

Each deserves its own chapter.

15. Technologists

Technologists design the organization's products and services. They are the engineers at all layers, the analysts and professional specialists, the designers and the gurus.

Technologists maintain a locus of expertise in an engineering discipline, technology, or product line; and they use their expertise to design, build, repair, and support solutions.

In more complex functions and industries, there are two major categories of Technologists: Applications and Base.

Applications Technologists produce *purpose-specific products.*

Applications may be built from a variety of components, and may be built on top of a variety of platforms. These components and platforms are termed "Base Technologies."

Base Technologists are specialists in disciplines and technologies that are *not purpose-specific.*

For example, civil engineers are Applications Technologists; they build bridges. They employ a wide variety of Base Technologies, such as stress engineers, electrical engineers, and traffic engineers, who contribute parts and advice.

In a corporate example, Applications Technologists are the engineers who design the company's ultimate products, like cars. They employ Base Technologists who design engines, suspensions, interiors, manufacturing processes, etc.

In IS, for an example of an internal support function, the term "application" refers to data-specific software, systems designed to handle information about a particular topic. Base Technologists sell and support computing, database, and telecommunications platforms; end-user computing tools; software-engineering tools and methods; and information-handling disciplines such as artificial intelligence.

Technologists sell and install products, often utilizing external product vendors as extensions to their staff. They also enhance, tune, repair, replace, and support their products.

Note that this definition does not distinguish those who build from those who repair. Essentially the same professional expertise is required to do both: a knowledge of the design of the organization's product line.

If you drill down to the next level of detail, you'll see with greater resolution the products and professional specialties. But as you drill down, never split this building block by tasks, methods, tools, or any subset of the services offered by Technologists.

For example, in IS, applications technologists can be divided into groups based on the applications (objects) they support, but should never be divided by tasks such as development versus maintenance.

In summary, the domains of Technologists are based on their specialties, defined in terms of expertise in a specific range of products.

16. Service Bureaus

Service Bureaus keep things running. They provide ongoing services reliably and efficiently. This building block includes manufacturing, customer service, and the range of support services.

There are two types of Service Bureaus: Machine-based, which own and operate infrastructure to provide services to others; and People-based which provide ongoing support services which are produced by people rather than the infrastructure itself.

Machine-based Service Bureaus own and operate shared-use infrastructure. (The word "machine" is intended in the most metaphorical sense, to include hardware, software, and information.) The services they sell are based on access to their infrastructure; the people are there to ensure that the machines run properly.

In a corporation, this is the manufacturing function. In IS, this includes the computer center, telecommunications network operations, and the telephone system.

Machine-based Service Bureaus buy the equipment in their factories (from Technologists). They own and operate this equipment to produce services for others. They are not experts in the design of the equipment; instead, they're expert in operating it to produce their services.

The contrast between Technologists and Machine-based Service Bureaus is illustrated by Boeing versus American Airlines, and Sun Microsystems versus America Online.

Machine-based Service Bureaus adjust the parameters built into the solutions they own, and follow procedures for their use and problem resolution. But if any changes to the design of the infrastructure are needed, Machine-based Service Bureaus buy help from Technologists.

People-based Service Bureaus provide *services produced by people rather than machines*. Equipment, such as computers, is employed only to make the people more productive at tasks they conceivably could do manually.

There are three types of functions which are categorized as People-based Service Bureaus:

1. Services to clients that enhance the organization's primary product line. The most common example is customer service (help desk or hotline).

2. Services to others within the organization to leverage their time and enhance their abilities. Examples include project management advice, field technicians that act on behalf of other product lines, and administrative services.

3. The organization may also include a few other relatively small functions that can be considered support to staff. These are entire businesses within a business that produce goods and services not specifically related to the organization's product line. Examples include procurement, education services, departmental finance, and departmental human resources.

This third type of People-based Service Bureau offers a product line that's outside the mainstream of the organization. It doesn't directly produce the products and services which the organization sells to its clients. Its role is indirect; it helps others in the organization produce their product lines. And, although it includes specialists in other disciplines, it is still considered a People-based Service Bureau rather than a Technologist.

Type-three People-based Service Bureaus are independent lines of business, and may be large enough to include all of the building blocks. Nonetheless, from the perspective of the organization in question, they are considered People-based Service Bureaus.

As much as Technologists love change — good ones will pursue with excitement every new product that comes along — Service Bureaus are the opposite. Responsible for stability, responsiveness, reliability, security, low cost, and attention to detail, they change only when it's safe.

Service Bureaus seek continuous improvements on the margin, but are not generally proponents of major changes which disrupt their operational efficiency.

Service Bureaus provide the operational foundation for the organization.

As you drill down in the structure, Service Bureaus are divided by the services they offer. In manufacturing, for example, groups can specialize in making certain products, but jobs should not be defined by tasks on an assembly line (the difference between teams that make cars and individuals on a line that do repetitive tasks).

17. Coordinators

The next building block, Coordinators, helps others within the organization, at least in part by helping them come to agreement with one another.

Coordinators help people individually by offering expertise and methods. In this way, they're like People-based Service Bureaus. Coordinators maintain an expertise in something other than the organization's products and services, and supply supporting products and services to customers, primarily with the organization itself.

But in the case of Coordinators, one key aspect of serving peers is helping them agree with one another where consistency among peers is required. In addition to contributing their own expertise, Coordinators facilitate a consensus of stakeholders on issues within their domain. This is the "coordinating" aspect of their work.

A common example is business strategy planning (deciding what business the organization should be in, and what it needs to do to get there).

Ideally, every entrepreneur in the organization develops a business strategy for his or her business within a business. But since strategic planning is a profession in its own right, the various managers may not be experts in developing business strategies. The Business Planning Coordinator supplies that expertise.

But in addition, everyone's individual strategies must plug together to form the organization's strategy. This is why coordination is needed.

The Business Planning Coordinator supplies a common set of environmental assumptions, formats, and time frames; and then ensures that people throughout the organization collaborate to come up with integrated, synergistic strategies.

There are a number of types of Coordinators, including the following:

* **Business planning:** Described above.

* **Organizational effectiveness:** Facilitates improvements in how the organization does business, including its culture, structure, internal economy, and metrics. Also coordinates employee communications.

* **Standards:** Sometimes called the "architect," builds consensus on constraints on product design that facilitate future integration and support.

* **Business continuity:** Facilitates planning for disaster recovery and continuing to do business through catastrophic events, the testing of those plans, and ultimately the exercise of those plans if needed.

* **Security policies:** Facilitates agreement on policies that make the business safer from espionage, theft, and sabotage. Also coordinates investigations of problems.

* **Design:** Helps multiple Technologist groups understand their technical interdependences (mapping the "ripples"), and coordinating their parallel projects.

* **Research:** Helps staff develop research proposals; helps the executive manage limited research funds and the portfolio of research projects such that everybody's research fits the business plan; and helps staff perform research.

Although similar in that they are coordination and facilitation functions, each of these types of Coordinators entails unique backgrounds and skills, and each is a profession (a line of business, i.e., a building block at the next level of detail) in its own right.

18. Consultancies

Consultancies comprise the sales and marketing functions. They provide the link between clients' business needs and the organization's products and services.

Everyone knows that a company needs a sales and marketing organization. But many internal service departments lack an equivalent function.

While people may not like the thought of sales internal to the company, this building block is absolutely critical to every internal support function. It's the one that spends most of its time with clients, getting to know the people and the business issues. It helps clients discover their needs for its products, linking the organization to clients' business strategies. It helps peers within the organization understand clients and their needs. And it facilitates healthy relationships between clients and the rest of the organization.

Strategic alignment is a key deliverable of this building block. Consultants do more than act as client liaisons and broker projects with other groups within the organization. They diagnose clients' business strategies and link mission-critical opportunities to the right subset of the organization's products and services. In this way, Consultants translate clients' strategic business opportunities into "sales" for the organization. [3]

Although many internal support functions leave this critical function to their senior managers to perform in their spare time, it deserves a separate place on the organization chart for three reasons:

First, to align itself with its clients' business strategies, an organization must be prepared to flexibly offer any subset of its products

---

3.   A business within a business "sells" its products and services to internal clients, whether or not money changes hands. Ultimately, clients pay for what they get, whether via the organization's budget or through fee-for-service chargebacks.

and services as required by the business challenge of the day. But it's not easy to be business driven when you're also a provider of a specific subset of the product line.

Therefore, to build strategic alignment, organizations need a business-oriented professional who is independent of any of its specific product lines.

Second, the Consultancy requires a unique set of skills. Consider the job requirements of the Consultancy:

* An understanding of the clients' business strategies (e.g., an M.B.A. degree and industry experience). Knowledge of the clients' organization, and the political savvy to determine which clients are most critical to strategy and, hence, most worth serving. The ability to talk to these key client executives about issues of critical concern.

* In-depth understanding of how to identify the key concerns and needs of these strategic clients; i.e., methods to diagnose high-payoff, strategic requirements (sometimes called "counselor selling").

* A broad awareness of all of the products of the organization plus a lack of technical bias, to permit purely business-driven recommendations of the solutions most appropriate to clients' needs. Any product bias whatsoever will lead to a technology-driven "solution-in-search-of-a-problem" approach.

* Excellent interpersonal skills to build healthy relations between clients and everyone in the organization.

* Behavioral skills such as interviewing, listening, mediation, and negotiation; and knowledge of participative change management methods that ensure effective implementation of the organization's products.

* Knowledge of finance, decision science, economics, and policy analysis to measure value-added (strategic) benefits. This is

needed to justify and to evaluate solutions that generate strategic value.

*   Sufficient time to spend with clients and involvement in their business so as to be readily accessible and considered part of the client's management team.

As capable as senior managers may be, they are ill equipped to do the Consultancy function. They are busy people who don't have sufficient time to spend walking the clients' halls, attending clients' management meetings, and discussing everything from business strategies to specific projects.

Third, managers are focused on other functions, and have little time or energy to perfect the business-driven Consulting methods such as needs assessment and benefits measurement.

The Consultancy should be separate from the Service Bureaus (including from customer service functions). The Consultancy is focused on new adventures — it mustn't get bogged down in day-to-day operational responsibilities. Those who are busy fighting fires don't have time to discover new opportunities.

Similarly, the Consultancy should be separate from Technologists. Their perspective is the opposite of Technologists': Consultants are generalists in products and specialists in their clients' business; Technologists are specialists in their respective products, but generalists with regard to who uses them.

So the message is: The Consultancy function should be respected as a building block in its own right, even within internal service provider organizations.

There are four types of Consultancies:

*   **Account:** high-level account representatives who are the default points of contact for a set of clients (their territory). They produce a stream of strategic opportunities by serving key opinion-leading clients with comprehensive strategic analyses. They are proactive, and do a lot for the few. In a

company, they are a direct sales force for major accounts. In an internal service provider department, they are the liaisons with client business units.

*   **Function:** experts in the clients' professions, available to help Account Consultants (in any territory) with business analyses. While the Account Consultant is the primary representative to a client business unit, when working in, say, the procurement and manufacturing areas, the Account Consultancy may call in a Function Consultant who specializes in supply-chain issues to help diagnose their strategic requirements.

*   **Retail:** available to anyone on demand for business advice and unbiased business diagnoses. They are reactive, and do a little for the many. They are analogous to a retail store for walk-in clients. They may even manage a showroom or demonstration center.

*   **Marketing:** the one-to-many functions that coordinate communications with the client community, for example, with brochures, newsletters, awareness events, and public relations. They also offer peers within the organization help with marketing planning. And they offer market research services which answer questions about what groups of clients think (e.g., customer satisfaction surveys).

In all its forms, Consultancies facilitate partnerships with clients, and link clients' business challenges to the organization's various products and services.

19. Audit

The final building block is Audit.

Many organizations include an Audit function, but their role is often controversial and confused.

Audit is not the same as quality inspection. In the spirit of total quality management, quality inspection is the responsibility of every producing function. It should be done every day in the normal course of doing business, not occasionally by outsiders. (This point was made in Chapter 11.)

Rather, Audit performs *periodic checks to ensure that people are complying with rules and policies*. It judges the work of others on behalf of someone other than the people being judged.

Audit involves problem identification, not problem diagnosis and repair. Auditors should never make suggestions for corrective actions. To do so would be exercising undue influence, a conflict of interests. Imagine if the Internal Revenue Service recommended a particular vendor's general ledger system! Auditors' focus should be strictly on examining results, not recommending solutions.

Auditors check on compliance; they do not replace managers by setting objectives, giving orders, or measuring results.

Audit should never be used to substitute for direction through line management. The order to comply with rules and policies must come through one's chain of command to have legitimacy, as should the directive to cooperate with Auditors. Without such legitimacy, Auditors will have a difficult time doing their jobs, and compliance will be minimal.

Audit is not only a distinct building block of structure. It must be kept entirely separate from the other service-oriented functions. It is impossible for the same people to both serve and police others, and any fulfillment of the Audit function compromises a group's ability to be customer focused and to partner with those it serves. Imagine someone saying, "I'm from the Internal Revenue Service. I'd like to help you with your financial planning!"

While Auditors can be polite and professional, they sell their services to stakeholders other than those whom they audit.

ASSEMBLING THE
BUILDING BLOCKS

20. Diagnosing Your Structure:
The Rainbow Exercise

The framework of building blocks presented in the last section can be used in two ways: to diagnose potential problems in an organization chart; and to design an optimal organization chart.

Let's start with how to examine an organization chart, real or proposed, and anticipate the dysfunctions — the ways in which the structure will get in the way of people's performance.

Then, in the next chapter, we'll convert these observations into practical guidelines for combining the building blocks into a healthy organization chart.

For reasons that will become obvious, we call this diagnostic process the "rainbow exercise." It's meant to be done collaboratively by the leadership team of an organization, as a consensus-building process.

First, enlarge and post the organization chart. And get a set of eight or more colored marker pens.

Put a red stripe under any box that's doing Consultancy work; a blue stripe under Applications Technologists and purple under Base Technologists; and so on.

In other words, color code the organization chart, identifying which building blocks fall within each box. (If you're analyzing the current organization, be honest and color code the organization chart based on what people actually do, regardless of what they're supposed to do.)

Once the color coding is completed, look at your colorful chart for four types of problems: gaps, rainbows, scattered campuses, and inappropriate substructures. (See Figure 2.)

* **Gaps:** where a function is missing altogether, or is performed part-time by people whose primary focus is something else. (Look for a missing color, or for a color spread around the charts in combination with other colors.) Gaps lead to:

   - **Lack of professional excellence:** With no one looking after the function as their primary focus, there is no focal point for accumulating experience, and no one has time to study and evolve world-class methods. This leads to poor quality, and a lack of innovation.

   - **Unreliable processes:** When a function is not receiving anyone's primary attention, it is not likely to be a reliable process. People do it when they have time, "catch as catch can." Continual improvement in the process is also unlikely, since people think of the function only when they need to, if at all.

* **Rainbows:** where a group is expected to perform more than one function. (Look for groups marked with more than one color.) Rainbows lead to two potential problems:

   - **Impossible requisite variety:** When building blocks are combined, the resulting job requires a much greater diversity of skills, exceeding most people's variety-handling abilities. In other words, people are expected to be experts at too many things and feel stretched too thinly. As a result, they may be mediocre at many of their assignments, and may neglect other duties altogether.

   - **Conflicts of interests:** When people are asked to pursue conflicting objectives, serious performance problems result. In particular, the combination of Technologists and Service Bureaus (innovation versus operations), and Technologists and Consultancy (bias of the product specialist versus an unbiased diagnosis of the business), lead to poor results at one of the two functions.

* **Scattered campuses:** when a function is spread around the organization. (Look for a color common to more than one group.) Scattered campuses raise the following concerns:

   - **Loss of the campus effect:** Professional exchange among peers within a specialty is reduced, so people are less likely to learn from each other and exchange tricks of the trade. This slows the pace of learning and innovation, and reduces productivity and quality.

   - **Product-line disintegration:** It is difficult to get like experts to agree upon standards and common products. Each pocket of the profession is likely to establish its own culture, practices, and standards; so product fragmentation develops. Also, a variety of different brands and styles of the same product may compete for clients' attention.

   - **Overlapping territories:** If no single manager is responsible for allocating domains within a building block, then there is no one person whose job is to ensure that every topic is covered in one and only one place.

   Expertise in a specialty may develop in one location and not be accessible to others. When it's needed elsewhere, the research is replicated. In time, overlaps develop, and two groups compete to deliver the same function. As a result, reinvention is common and productivity is diminished. Also, overlaps lead to territorial friction and confusion in the product line.

   - **Poor coverage:** Similarly, with no single manager looking after comprehensive coverage of the building block, it is difficult to be sure that every topic is covered somewhere. As a result, new technologies, techniques, and services may not be researched and supported. Since there is no guarantee that the organization's product line will remain comprehensive, opportunities may be lost.

*   **Inappropriate substructures:** where people are divided into groups based on something other than their specialty.

Structure tells people what they are supposed to be good at. If the basis for substructure is anything other than a building block's expertise, the following types of problems occur:

-   **Reduced specialization:** For example, a structure that dedicates groups to clients is right for the Account Consultancy function, but wrong for every other building block.

  If Technologists are substructured by client, specialization is reduced. Each client-dedicated group must cover the entire range of technologies and applications. All the generalists in each client-dedicated group must research the same professional topics, and develop overlapping product lines.

  Conversely, if the Account Consultancy is substructured by anything other than clients, each client would have to interface with more than one account representative, creating confusion and distance.

  Meanwhile, specialization in the clients' business is reduced. Instead of being dedicated to one client business unit, each Consultant would have to work with more than one on a portion of the issues. They'll come to know less about the clients, and take on more knowledge of the organization's products — that is, replicate the expertise of the Technologists.

-   **Biases:** For example, if Technologists are substructured by client and yet are still expected to be specialists in a particular product line, then clients will not get fair access to the organization's entire product set.

- **Fragmented jobs:** If Technologists are substructured by tasks (e.g., planning versus doing, or development versus maintenance), jobs are fragmented. Two groups become responsible for the same line of business, and no one will feel accountable for the product line. In addition, a poor motivational climate is likely to occur.

  If Coordinator functions are divided by anything other than that which they coordinate (e.g., standards, business plans, organizational effectiveness), the very purpose of coordination is defeated. Processes become fragmented, synergies are lost, and integrated results are unlikely.

  In Service Bureaus, there may be a tendency to define groups by tasks rather than by the services they offer. For example, jobs may be defined as steps on an assembly line, rather than responsibility for a set of products.

  Whole jobs give people responsibility for every aspect of a product line — a business within the business. A lack of whole jobs undermines empowerment, customer focus, and entrepreneurship.

Of course, good people who are willing to work very hard can overcome most structural dysfunctions. But wouldn't you rather they devote their energies to pleasing clients rather than overcoming self-imposed hurdles?

The rainbow exercise can tell a leadership team whether structural changes are needed. If they are, it helps leaders who are designing a new organization chart to anticipate the problems with a proposed structure before rolling out something they'll later regret.

21. Designing a High-performance Structure

Now, on to a more positive topic: how to design healthy, high-performance organization charts.

First, let's revisit the requirements of a healthy design that were summarized in Chapter 4:

*   Provide every group with clear domains.

*   Ensure that all possible product lines are included.

*   Ensure no overlaps (no internal competition) by providing every group with a distinct domain.

*   Structure by specialty.

*   Distinguish customers from bosses.

*   Structure to deliver what customers ask of you, not as customers wish you to structure.

*   Give every group a future.

*   Give people whole, empowered jobs.

Note that every one of these requirements can be satisfied when you design an organization chart using the building blocks.

In fact, many are satisfied by the very definition of the building blocks:

*   Each building block is clearly defined.

*   Each building block is a line of business; a whole job with responsibility for everything to do with its business within a business. It's defined based on its products; not based on clients' organizational structures, or based on customer's motives for buying its products.

*   Jobs are empowered, since they're defined by what the group sells, not what people do or how they produce their products and services.

*   No building block is in business to control another, to decide how another does business, or to put another out of business.

*   Each building block contains a minimum in conflicts of interests.

But other requirements are satisfied (or not) based on how the building blocks are combined.

To guide the process of combining building blocks into organization charts, the four questions of the rainbow exercise can be inverted into positive principles:

*   **Gaps:** A full-service organization includes all of the functional building blocks. If any are missing, critical activities will not occur with reliability and quality.

    Ensure that responsibility for every building block is placed somewhere in the new organization chart, whether or not it's a full-time job.

    This does not mean that every building block must be staffed with permanent resources, whether or not demand for its services exists. It simply means that someone must be accountable for every line of business, whether it be fulfilled by one's own staff or contractors. That manager can then select and supervise contractors, and build staff as workload warrants.

*   **Rainbows:** Don't combine building blocks unless you have strong business reasons (no rainbows).

    Designing a job that's responsible for multiple building blocks inevitably creates impossible requisite variety, and generally creates conflicts of interests. The result is lower performance.

Thus, it is best to separate the building blocks (with their conflicting objectives), ideally leaving only the organization's executive responsible for more than one.

Reserving inevitable conflicts of interests for the highest possible level of the organization has a number of advantages. It ensures that the most seasoned leaders, those with the broadest strategic purview, deal with the difficult balancing acts involved in paradoxical objectives such as innovation versus operational stability.

It also separates conflicting forces so that the executive can explicitly adjust the balances among them.

Focusing jobs on a single functional building block also sends a clear message to everybody in the organization about their roles and their relationships to each other and to clients. Excellence comes from focusing on one subject area in great depth.

Clearly focused jobs also help people understand what others in the organization offer, building a basis for collaboration.

Generally, the impulse to create rainbows can be addressed through better teamwork among specialists.

*   **Scattered campuses:** Keep all related lines of business (each high-level building block) together under a common boss. The job of this boss is to cultivate the function, and to ensure that the domain is covered completely and without overlaps.

*   **Inappropriate substructure:** Layer by layer, divide people up based on the building block's product line, i.e., based on their specialty. The nature of each building block determines the appropriate basis for structure within that part of the organization.

The building blocks recommend what some would call a "functional structure." In the past few decades it has been fashionable to criticize functional structures for lacking customer focus and discouraging collaboration (i.e., building "stovepipes").

Alternatives, such as customer-aligned and matrix structures, have been tried. As you've read, for the most part, these have created more problems than they've solved. The problems of poor customer focus and collaboration are real; but the structural answers that were tried were misguided.

There is no inherent reason why a functional structure cannot be customer focused. In fact, a structure built on lines of business (both internal and external) is inherently customer focused. And effective teamwork across boundaries can be built (or not built) in any structure. (The mechanics of high-performance teamwork are the subject of the next section in this book.)

Nonetheless, there is a natural tendency to put people under a common boss because they work together frequently. It requires a leap of faith to design an organization chart that bets on cross-boundary teamwork. But if a leadership team wants to build a very high-performance organization, that's the right thing to do.

So instead of considering who works with whom, consider the various types of synergies that occur when similar building blocks are structured side by side:

*   **Business synergies:** put similar businesses together to avoid redundancies; maximize economies of scale; encourage reuse of products.

*   **Professional synergies:** put similar professions together to encourage reuse of competencies through the exchange of knowledge (the campus effect).

*   **Management synergies:** reduce difficult domain boundaries to the lowest possible level; focus management attention, coaching, and career development on a single professional area.

*   **Cultural synergies:** create a consistent sub-culture appropriate

to the building block (e.g., service through people, operation of machines, purpose-specific solutions, highly specialized technical knowledge, knowledge of clients, facilitation and coordination, policing).

*   **Appropriate bias:** develop a single bias (specialty) in each group, and especially avoid conflicts of interests.

Additionally, as you're dividing building blocks at the next level of the organization, you'll have to consider span of control. The number of subordinates that a manager can supervise is a function of variety — which is a product of both volume and complexity.

Span can be greater in functions that do a lot of volume in a set of similar products; conversely, where there's a lot of diversity in the product line, even if the volume of work or number of people is less, span may have to be more narrow.

The actual structure that each organization develops will vary based on the range of technologies, size of the organization, stage of growth, skills, culture, and focus. Each organization must determine its own unique set of businesses, using the functional building blocks as a precise language for design and the principles as guidelines for assembling them.

22. Domains

To have any meaningful effect, a structural design must be documented in more detail than a few words in a box on a chart. A structure is best manifested in a set of "domains" — clear definitions of the boundaries within which each group sells its products and services.

Documenting clear domains has a number of valuable benefits:

*   Clear boundaries head off territorial disputes.

*   Clear lines of business specify who does what on every project.

*   If domains are open-ended, they determine where accountability for anything new (e.g., researching new products) fits in the structure.

Once the organization chart is decided, domains can be written for each group in the structure. (A group may write more than one domain if it's designed as a rainbow.) Domain statements may be as simple as a single sentence, or may be a paragraph or page in length.

Writing clear domains is a science in itself.

The most important aspect of a domain is a clear definition of the boundaries within which the group works. Ask: "What makes this group different from its peers?" or "What is its territory?"

Together, all the groups' domains must add up to the total domain of the organization — that is, they must be comprehensive. And, of course, there must be no overlap in any two groups' domains.

Beyond the obvious caution to avoid overlaps and gaps, the following guidelines apply to wording domains:

*   **Focus on what you sell, not what you do.** It's important that the language be consistent with an entrepreneurial focus on results, not tasks. Phrases such as "act as" and "responsible for" which describe tasks and bureaucratic territories rather than deliverables should be avoided. Instead of saying "responsible for," it's better to say "sells all products which...."

*   **Describe your product line at a general level; don't list the individual products.** Domains should not list individual products and services, and should not mention specific models or brands (which quickly become obsolete).

    Instead, domains should include a generic description of the types of products offered. For example, the domain of an Applications Technologists group should be specified in terms such as "all products whose primary intent is to achieve the purpose of..." rather than by a list of current products.

    Defining domains in terms of general rules is important for two reasons: It clarifies where each new technology fits within the organization, so as not to subject the organization to repeated territorial questions every time new services are offered or product models evolve. And it gives each group room to grow their business with creative new product offerings, as long as it stays within its domain.

    Furthermore, when done this way, domains should not require updating repeatedly as the product set evolves.

*   **Describe your product line by defining clear rules.** For example, say: "We sell any products that meet the following criteria...."

    Technologists, for example, sell any products that require in-depth expertise in the design of the organization's primary products.

Consultants sell all products that require a generalist's understanding of the organization's products, and a deep understanding of clients and their businesses. Within that, Account Consultants define their domains in terms of which clients each serves (their sales territories).

* **Choose criteria that match the group's "basis for substructure."**

The criteria might be the nature of the group's expertise.

For example, Technologists' domains should explain exactly which technologies are covered by each group. Applications Technologists define the class of products handled by each group. For Base Technologists, domains generally bound the technologies or design discipline.

Service Bureaus' and Coordinators' domains describe their services.

In writing a domain, only restrictions should be listed. A group that does every aspect of a given criterion (e.g., every geography) should either not mention it at all, or should specify that it satisfies *all* of that criterion.

* **Choose criteria that describe the products, not the circumstance of the sale.** Don't define domains based on customers' motives for buying (e.g., products that clients use to do this), or by the timing of the sale (e.g., at this stage of the process). Such criteria lead to a product falling within more than one domain, depending on circumstances.

With that said, it is acceptable to describe a class of products in terms of its design; for example, one might say, "any products whose primary intent is...."

At each level, the boss's domain is the basis for defining the domains at the next level. As you drill down the organization chart, the boss's domain is simply divided among subordinates.

For example, the domain of a Base Technologist (e.g., component engineering) executive might include all products which are not purpose specific. Within that high-level group, each manager's domain would bound a subset of those products.

Similarly, in a Machine-based Service Bureau, the high-level executive might be responsible for all services based on the ownership and operation of infrastructure. The managers within the group would define their domains in terms of the subset of services they offer.

In this way, domains are comprehensive (summing to the total product line of the organization) and discrete (without overlaps). And at each level, domains are divided based on the expertise and products of the function, ensuring whole jobs throughout the organization.

HIGH-PERFORMANCE TEAMWORK

23. What Is High-performance Teamwork?

If groups can't team, they can't specialize.

If you can't get help from your peers, you're forced to replicate their skills and muddle through on your own. When this happens, it doesn't matter what the organization chart says. Groups inevitably evolve into stovepipes of self-sufficient generalists.

Therefore, insightful leaders who structure their organization on the premise of specialization had best be prepared to invest in the mechanisms of teamwork.

This section addresses how to induce fluid, cross-boundary work flows so that an organization chart with clear and distinct domains actually works.

Teamwork means more than just a willingness to work together. Consider the requirements of high-performance teamwork: Teams must form quickly, and combine just the right specialized skills to address the challenge at hand. And effective collaboration depends on teams that work well without a lot of management intervention.

In other words, teams should be both *self-forming* and *self-managing*.

Self-forming means two things:

*   First, teams should form without the need for executive intervention. An organization cannot afford to wait for top management to decide when teams are needed and who should be on them. Executives cannot possibly know every collaborative relationship needed throughout the organization. Peers should be able to form teams laterally, without having to go up and back down the chain of command to talk to a peer.

*   Second, teams should involve just the right people at just the right time. Instead of team members being designated for the

life of a project, people arrive as needed, and leave the team when their unique contribution is delivered.

Self-managing also means two things:

* First, a healthy team doesn't wait for the top project manager to call all the shots. Team members should know their individual accountabilities and manage their own piece of the project to achieve their deliverables. "All for one and one for all" may sound nice, and may indeed work if all of the team members are generalists. But in teams of specialists, differentiating people's deliverables is essential.

* Second, once responsibilities are delineated, the team must somehow ensure that the various pieces of its work come together to produce the whole product. Furthermore, disputes should be handled within the team. This requires a clear chain of command within the team.

While the challenge of high-performance teamwork is not trivial, the answer is conceptually simple: the business-within-a-business paradigm.

Here's how it works: When new projects or services arise, a "prime contractor" is chosen based on clear domains.

The first job of the prime contractor is to line up subcontractors, who sell to the prime contractor either their time or specific deliverables. By examining others' domains, the prime can spot subcomponents that are better bought from the appropriate experts than done by the prime contractor's own group.

People have an incentive to draw others onto their project teams because entrepreneurs are more competitive when they utilize the services of specialized subcontractors rather than attempt to do everything themselves.

And people want to help each other since internal customers are customers nonetheless, and it's important to please them.

Since everyone who takes on a project is responsible for identifying his or her subcontractors, teams are assembled without the need for management intervention. In other words, teams are spontaneously *self-forming*.

When every prime and subcontractor buys from peers whatever help is needed, each team combines the right mix of specialists, across organizational boundaries — i.e., just the right people at just the right time.

And when groups buy *deliverables* from one another rather than just people's time — things like modules to build into the product, or studies and advice — then everybody on the team has clear individual accountabilities.

Of course, the notion of a prime, subs, and subs to subs creates a clear chain of command within the team.

As a result, teams are *self-managing,* and can make decisions and resolve disputes within the team.

Note that, in this paradigm, project management becomes much more feasible. Those who assume that one person can coordinate the detailed tasks of every involved discipline find themselves on a hopeless search for a small band of exceptional project managers.

Instead, if each layer only manages its subcontractors, the challenge of project management is shared by everyone on the project team. Each group that's accountable for delivering its products and services is a project manager for its subcomponents of the prime contract.

The business-within-a-business paradigm is not just a good model for designing organization charts. It also provides the basis for flexible, dynamic cross-boundary teamwork.

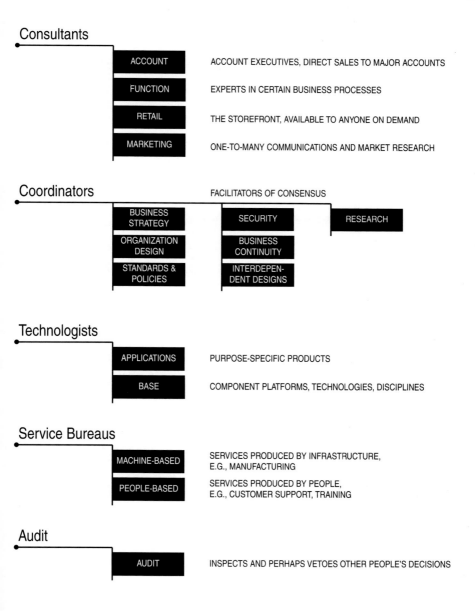

Consultants

ACCOUNT	ACCOUNT EXECUTIVES, DIRECT SALES TO MAJOR ACCOUNTS
FUNCTION	EXPERTS IN CERTAIN BUSINESS PROCESSES
RETAIL	THE STOREFRONT, AVAILABLE TO ANYONE ON DEMAND
MARKETING	ONE-TO-MANY COMMUNICATIONS AND MARKET RESEARCH

Coordinators

FACILITATORS OF CONSENSUS

BUSINESS STRATEGY	SECURITY	RESEARCH
ORGANIZATION DESIGN	BUSINESS CONTINUITY	
STANDARDS & POLICIES	INTERDEPEN-DENT DESIGNS	

Technologists

APPLICATIONS	PURPOSE-SPECIFIC PRODUCTS
BASE	COMPONENT PLATFORMS, TECHNOLOGIES, DISCIPLINES

Service Bureaus

MACHINE-BASED	SERVICES PRODUCED BY INFRASTRUCTURE, E.G., MANUFACTURING
PEOPLE-BASED	SERVICES PRODUCED BY PEOPLE, E.G., CUSTOMER SUPPORT, TRAINING

Audit

AUDIT	INSPECTS AND PERHAPS VETOES OTHER PEOPLE'S DECISIONS

issue $\longrightarrow$ problem $\longrightarrow$ symptom

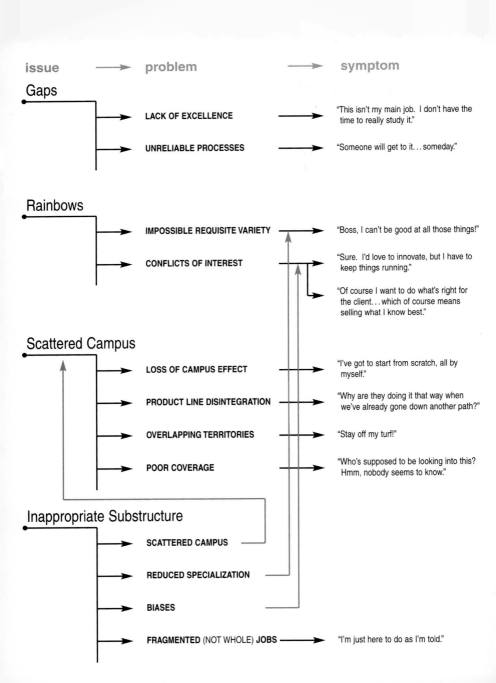

Gaps

LACK OF EXCELLENCE → "This isn't my main job. I don't have the time to really study it."

UNRELIABLE PROCESSES → "Someone will get to it...someday."

Rainbows

IMPOSSIBLE REQUISITE VARIETY → "Boss, I can't be good at all those things!"

CONFLICTS OF INTEREST → "Sure. I'd love to innovate, but I have to keep things running."

"Of course I want to do what's right for the client...which of course means selling what I know best."

Scattered Campus

LOSS OF CAMPUS EFFECT → "I've got to start from scratch, all by myself."

PRODUCT LINE DISINTEGRATION → "Why are they doing it that way when we've already gone down another path?"

OVERLAPPING TERRITORIES → "Stay off my turf!"

POOR COVERAGE → "Who's supposed to be looking into this? Hmm, nobody seems to know."

Inappropriate Substructure

SCATTERED CAMPUS

REDUCED SPECIALIZATION

BIASES

FRAGMENTED (NOT WHOLE) **JOBS** → "I'm just here to do as I'm told."

Name of Group **CUSTOMER**	
CLIENTS:	PRODUCT NAME 1 PRODUCT NAME 2 PRODUCT NAME 3
CONSULTANTS:	PRODUCT NAME 4 PRODUCT NAME 5 PRODUCT NAME 6
TECHNOLOGISTS:	PRODUCT NAME 1 PRODUCT NAME 6 PRODUCT NAME 7
STANDARDS COORDINATOR:	PRODUCT NAME 1 PRODUCT NAME 8 PRODUCT NAME 9
PLANNING COORDINATOR:	PRODUCT NAME 1 PRODUCT NAME 10
ORGANIZATIONAL EFFECTIVENESS:	PRODUCT NAME 1 PRODUCT NAME 11
MACHINE-BASED SERVICE BUREAUS:	PRODUCT NAME 1 PRODUCT NAME 7
PEOPLE-BASED SERVICE BUREAUS:	PRODUCT NAME 1 PRODUCT NAME 12

Name of Group **SUPPLIER**	
CLIENTS:	PRODUCT NAME 1 PRODUCT NAME 2 PRODUCT NAME 13
CONSULTANTS:	PRODUCT NAME 1 PRODUCT NAME 14 PRODUCT NAME 15
TECHNOLOGISTS:	PRODUCT NAME 1 PRODUCT NAME 16 PRODUCT NAME 17
STANDARDS COORDINATOR:	PRODUCT NAME 1 PRODUCT NAME 18 PRODUCT NAME 19
PLANNING COORDINATOR:	PRODUCT NAME 1 PRODUCT NAME 19
ORGANIZATIONAL EFFECTIVENESS:	PRODUCT NAME 1 PRODUCT NAME 20
MACHINE-BASED SERVICE BUREAUS:	PRODUCT NAME 1 PRODUCT NAME 21 PRODUCT NAME 22
PEOPLE-BASED SERVICE BUREAUS:	PRODUCT NAME 1 PRODUCT NAME 23

Steps in the Implementation Process

1. Tier-one candidates design tier-one structure.

2. The executive selects tier-one leaders.

3. Tier-one leaders define their domains.

4. Tier-one leaders develop their charters and practice walk-throughs.

5. Tier-one leaders draft tier-two structure.

6. Tier-two candidates are educated and contribute to tier-two structure.

7. Tier-one leaders select tier-two leaders.

8. Tier-two leaders define their domains.

9. Tier-two leaders develop their charters and practice walk-throughs.

10. All leaders plan the announcement and migration process.

11. All leaders roster all staff.

12. All leaders announce the new structure to all staff and provide education.

13. Responsibilities are systematically migrated to the right domain.

24. Charters and Walk-throughs

As a business within a business, each and every group needs to have a clear understanding not only of its products but also of its internal customers and suppliers.

As sensible as this businesslike perspective is, for many people, it takes a significant paradigm shift before they view peers within the organization as customers and suppliers. This kind of cultural change doesn't happen by simply redesigning the organization chart. More explicit and tangible mechanisms are needed to ensure that the right people are on each project team.

A powerful mechanism for teamwork is embodied in *"charters."* (See Figure 3.) A charter is not a mission statement. Rather, it's made of two lists: the group's customers (both clients and others within the organization) and the products it sells to each; and the group's suppliers and the products it buys from each.

In charters, the word "product" refers to both products and services. A product is something that a customer will own or consume. Each product is defined in terms of its *deliverables,* not that tasks that go into making it.

And the words "buy" and "sell" are meant to refer to relationships, regardless of whether money actually changes hands.

Charters become the basis for "walk-throughs" that describe project teams. In a walk-through, a project is first assigned to a prime contractor based on domains. Then, using the supplier side of his or her charter, the prime contractor identifies needed sub-contractors. They, in turn, can consider their supplier lists and buy help from other peers.

As the project is discussed and each member of the project team buys help from peers, a tree-structured project plan emerges. It tells everyone exactly what they're to deliver, and to whom.

Before an organization chart is implemented, walk-throughs help a leadership team debug the structure, clarify boundaries, and rehearse teamwork.

After the new structure is implemented, walk-throughs provide a powerful process for initiating new projects and building service-delivery teams. They become the first step in project planning.

Charters are rich and flexible descriptions of all the many work flows and subcontracting relationships. They are not fixed, as in pre-defined business processes. Instead, for each project, the walk-through identifies the unique mix of skills needed, exactly what each group's deliverables are, and the chain of command (who's prime and who's sub).

In practice, documenting charters helps each entrepreneur build a sense of ownership of a piece of the organization's business. This fosters a high level of commitment.

Charters also have a powerful impact on an organization's culture. Clarifying what products each group produces builds an entrepreneurial spirit. Entrepreneurship is further reinforced by awareness of customers to be pleased, suppliers to be motivated, and competition ready to take over if internal staff are less than satisfactory.

Charters can also help managers measure results. Expanding on the concept of 360-degree reviews, performance appraisals can be based not only on the opinion of one's supervisor, but also on the satisfaction of a well-defined list of internal customers, and on the assessment of one's teamwork and project management skills by suppliers.

Most importantly, charters and walk-throughs have an incredibly positive effect on teamwork. They define boundaries to prevent territorial disputes, and specify interdependencies to encourage collaboration. Charters weave teamwork into the fabric of the organization.

IDEAS TO ACTION

25.   How to Implement a World-class Restructuring

How are restructurings usually done?

Quite often, the boss plays with boxes on paper, typically with the personalities of the senior managers in mind, until he or she has something that might work.

Or the senior management team plays with boxes for a few days until they agree, although it may not be clear what they're agreeing to since they all understand the boxes somewhat differently.

Then, lower level groups are assigned to the new top-level boxes, for the most part intact. A few obvious rainbows may be broken up.

Finally, the organization chart is published with fanfare, perhaps with some speeches that are intended to teach people the meaning of the new structure. And with that, senior management declares victory and the people are left to figure out how to make it work.

The result is a structure designed without the benefit of a precise language (such as the building blocks and domains), and without the guidance of science (the principles). It may solve a few problems while creating many more.

Furthermore, it may assume teamwork, but it does nothing to raise the organization's ability to form cross-boundary workflows (no charters and walk-throughs).

The combination of limited involvement and unclear language means that people in the organization will have limited and varying understandings of what was intended. And with the same old constraints on teamwork, people still have to do whatever it takes to get their jobs done, building stovepipes in spite of what the organization chart says.

As a result, typically little changes. People fall back into old patterns of work... until a year or two later, when the organization repeats the entire process.

Hence the justifiable cynicism about reorganizations.

There is a better way....

Every organization is unique. That's why each organization's structure has to be tailored to its unique culture, business, and people. This book isn't going to suggest an "off the shelf" organization chart that applies to any and all organizations.

In fact, it's just the opposite. The concepts in this book are intended to help those who must live within the organization to design it, and in the process, understand it as a dynamic system.

So far, this book has introduced three tools essential to effective restructurings: the building blocks, the principles described with the rainbow exercise for assembling the building blocks into a structure, and the mechanisms of high-performance teamwork that are necessary for people to remain within their domains.

There are two more ingredients to success, both attributes of the structural change process: participation, and planning.

First, *participation*. This means more than some involvement of the top few senior managers. A successful restructuring is based on widespread participation of the entire management team, and ultimately, of everyone in the organization. Like a barn raising, the community works together to design and implement the kind of organization in which people want to work.

Participation is important for at least four reasons:

One, it brings the detailed knowledge of "the way things really work around here" into the design process. The few senior managers at the top can't possibly know the organization as well as the collection of all managers. The diversity of experiences, perspectives, and insights of the whole management team add a richness to the process, and ensure that the resulting design is comprehensive and feasible.

Two, participation induces understanding. A structure built around businesses within a business may be radically different from the culture of the past. Without a clear understanding of what business each group is in, managers won't see their jobs as all that different from the past. The boundaries may be a bit cleaner; but without participation, the restructuring is unlikely to deliver a customer-focused, entrepreneurial, team-oriented organization.

Three, when people understand the various lines of business within the organization, they become aware of the opportunity to buy from peers rather than dabble in other people's specialties in an attempt to be self-sufficient. Knowing what's available from peers counters the need for stovepipes and encourages teamwork.

Four, participation builds commitment. As in any significant change, the support of the people who must make it work is critical. Meaningful participation in the design of the new structure builds a sense of ownership and commitment.

Of course, the image of your entire management team — dozens, if not hundreds, of people — all in a room debating the boxes on an organization chart is absurd. Widespread participation must be carefully orchestrated.

To alleviate one concern, note that the building blocks and the principles provide a systematic basis for participation. They facilitate healthy contributions from everyone while avoiding a political "free for all" debate over opinions clouded by politics and personal interests.

Instead of the debate sounding like, "I want this," participants communicate in unambiguous terms (the building blocks), and they frame their arguments in light of the principles. For example, we've heard participants say, "combining these two building blocks creates a minor conflict of interests, but I think the synergies outweigh the risks."

Related to that, healthy contributions depend on people being open and objective. This is unlikely if people are worried about protecting their jobs or their turf.

We've found that three guarantees are necessary to create a safe environment conducive to open participation, and to elicit the maximum commitment to the new organization:

*   No one will lose compensation as a result of restructuring. If people fit best in lower-graded jobs, their compensation is protected, at least for a few years.

*   No one will lose their job as a result of restructuring. Any necessary headcount reductions should occur before (or well after) structural change. If job losses are blamed on the new structure, the new organization will be resented and not seen as a positive change leading to a healthy work environment for those who remain.

*   No one will be forced to relocate as a result of restructuring. If people fit best under a manager who lives elsewhere, they are managed remotely.

Another concern about widespread participation is the challenge of getting so many people to agree on a design. This can be manageable if the process is properly constructed.

A well-planned process takes the design team through a series of decisions, one at a time, each building on the last. For each decision, discussions are framed by the language of the building blocks and the principles of the rainbow exercise. Combine a structured process with good meeting process facilitation, and we've found that teams of 20 to 30 people can come to consensus on a new organizational structure in just a few days, building deep understanding and solid commitment along the way.

And that leads us to the second key ingredient of success: *planning*.

In a moment, I'll describe the process of design and implementation that's evolved over years of experiences, one that's benefited from the lessons provided by countless mistakes. But first, let me relate a story that illustrates the spirit of this planning process....

Noel Thomas, former strategic planner at a large steel company, tells of his visit to a Japanese steel mill to learn how they consistently delivered superior products at lower costs. Expecting to find exotic new technologies, instead he was surprised to find the same kind of mills and production processes as were used in North America.

After some study, he came to the following insight: In Japan, they spent (figuratively speaking) three months planning a new production line, two months building it, and one month commissioning it. In North America, companies typically spend one month planning, two months building, and then *years* trying to get the new facility to run well.

Noel's insight applies well to organizational restructuring.

You're no doubt familiar with the traditional approach to structural changes: the boss announces the new organization chart, and everyone spends years trying to get it to work right. This entails lots of confusion, evident to both staff and customers throughout the rest of the corporation. (And perhaps things start to settle into place just in time for the next reorganization.)

In our consulting practice, we've found the Japanese approach far more effective. We figure out exactly how the organization will work *before* it's announced.

Bringing the themes of participation and planning together, we use a "cascade" strategy to gain widespread involvement in planning the new organization. (See Figure 4.)

First, the pool of candidates for tier-one jobs (those who will be reporting directly to the top executive) study the building blocks and the principles, and design the tier-one structure. Then, a fair selection process chooses people for those jobs. Selecting from the pool of people who designed the new structure ensures a deep understanding of and commitment to the new organization.

This new tier-one leadership team plans the details of how the tier-one organization will work. They document clear domains. They develop their charters. And they practice walk-throughs until teamwork becomes second nature.

(Meanwhile, the old organization and leadership team remain in place and continue to run the business.)

With a solid understanding among the new tier-one leaders of how the new organization will work, the process cascades to tier two. In this phase, the tier-one leaders become the teaching team, and the tier-two candidates are involved in the design of tier-two structure.

To prime the pump, the tier-one leaders draft a tier-two structure, and bring in all the tier-two candidates to review their plans. This is typically a large group, but their input is carefully orchestrated in a two-day retreat.

Once the tier-two structure is finalized, a fair selection process assigns people to those jobs. Tier-one leaders make the selections as a team.

Once selected, the new tier-two leaders document their domains (dividing up their bosses' tier-one domains). Then, they split their bosses' charters into tier-two charters, and they practice walk-throughs until they all understand exactly how real work will be done in the new structure.

When any individual tier-one or tier-two leader is able, given a real-life project, to describe a walk-through in the same way that every other leader would, then finally the new structure and leadership team is ready for implementation.

Together, the tier-one and tier-two leaders plan the process by which the new structure will be announced and implemented, and roster the remaining staff. Staff are rostered based on what they do today, and where the best fit for them is in the new structure.

Finally, all tier-one and tier-two leaders together become the teaching team, and the process cascades to the rest of the organization. This roll-out and migration process is carefully planned to ensure effective and lasting change at every level of the organization with a minimum of disruption and risk.

By the way, announcement day isn't the first time that staff hear of the new structure. Open communication is fundamental to a successful change process. To ensure this, a communication plan is crafted at every step of the planning process.

This participative planning process requires significant effort, but pays off in an organization that is better in important ways: People throughout the organization feel vested in the new structure and empowered as entrepreneurs. They treat clients in a business-like manner, and treat each other as customers and suppliers. The result is an unbeatable combination of specialization, teamwork, and customer focus.

And as to the effort involved, if you count all the muddling around in public following the traditional pronouncement of a new organization chart, is this planned approach really more effort? Is it really slower?

Getting everyone to understand not just a new organization chart, but also a new way of doing business, takes time. It's a "pay me now, or pay me later" issue. In our experience, the participative, planned approach is far more effective.

And thanks to the time spent planning, the new organization "hits the ground running," fulfilling the promise of the new structure in weeks rather than years. It's another example of the tortoise beating the hare.

26. Adaptations for Small Organizations

Small organizations face all of the challenges of large organizations — diverse client needs, demand for technical excellence, the need for integration, and expectations of operational efficiency. They just have fewer resources with which to address them.

Small organizations may mistakenly assume that the Building Blocks Approach is too big and complex to apply to their limited headcount. This is not true! In fact, human nature and the principles of organizational design are precisely the same in large and small organizations.

In small organizations, however, some adaptations are appropriate.

Use of vendors and contractors will be more prevalent in small organizations, particularly in the area of Technologists. Specialists in less-used and emerging technologies are hired as contractors when needed.

However, someone in the organization must represent each functional building block, and be responsible for identifying and managing those contractors. This is termed "extended staffing," as distinct from outsourcing. [4]

Two functions are particularly strategic and require an insider's understanding of the company. Even in the smallest organization, Coordinators and Consultancies should never be delegated to contractors. If necessary, it is better for the organization's executive to fulfill these functions part time.

In small organizations, some combinations of building blocks are inevitable. People have to wear multiple "hats."

---

4.   For more on outsourcing, see: Meyer, N. Dean. *Outsourcing: how to make vendors work for your shareholders.*

While this may violate the principle of requisite variety, conflicts of interests can still be eliminated. The key is to combine responsibilities *within a building block* (for example, combining responsibility for a few different Technologist product lines), and *never across building blocks* (for example, never combining Technologists and Service Bureaus).

Small- to medium-sized organizations are likely to find a very flat structure (wide span of control) appropriate. For example, all of the Account Consultants and a supervisor of the Retail and Marketing Consultancies might report directly to the organization's executive.

In addition to these design considerations, in smaller organizations the implementation process (summarized in Chapter 25) can be simplified to skip the tier-two cascade since there are fewer layers of management involved.

With all the same challenges and even greater need to make the most of limited resources, small organizations are excellent candidates for the Building Blocks Approach.

27.   The Challenge of Leadership

Building a healthy organization is by far the most important and pressing responsibility facing any executive. And it's a highly leveraged use of an executive's time. By setting up an environment that sends the right signals, and then empowering and coaching people throughout the organization, the executive's vision can be translated into action many times over.

Structure is not a panacea, but it is one of the most powerful tools of leadership.

I hope this book has made it clear that structure is science, not art. It's a form of engineering. And understanding the science of structure should be considered a fundamental competency of leadership.

There are four key elements to the Building Blocks Approach:

1.   Clear definitions of the various functions within an organization — the building blocks of structure.

2.   Pragmatic principles for assembling the building blocks into an organization chart.

3.   Mechanisms for forming multi-disciplinary teams dynamically, i.e., charters and walk-throughs.

4.   A carefully planned implementation process that brings about paradigm shifts and dramatic cultural change along with a healthy structure in an open and participative manner.

The first two elements — the building blocks of structure and the principles of design — can be used to diagnose problems in an existing structure, or to design, from the ground up, a healthy structure.

The third element — work-flows, the flexible mechanisms of

teamwork — brings an organization chart to life by determining how work will get done.

The fourth element — the implementation process — is critical to making the design a reality.

Together, these four elements make up a science of organizational structure.

Using the Building Blocks Approach achieves a number of extremely important objectives:

* It allows executives to solve structural problems without creating new ones.

* It overcomes political biases, and allows organizations to take advantage of individual strengths without structuring around individual personalities.

* It helps executives communicate the various roles within the organization clearly to other leaders, clients, and the organization's staff. Clients better understand whom to call for what, and people throughout the organization better understand their roles and what it means to be excellent at their jobs.

* It makes it safe to open the design process to participation by people throughout the organization, shifting discussions from political combat to objective principles.

These are just a few of the many advantages of a scientific approach to organizational structure.

Unfortunately, it's not a simple science. To give you an idea of its depth, the study from which this book was drawn is well over 700 pages long!

Furthermore, its application to real organizations is not easy. People are naturally afraid of change, defensive about their territories, and reluctant to depend on others. As a result, restructuring processes tend to be challenging, both intellectually and emotionally.

But for leaders who are thoughtful and committed to doing what's right, the rewards are many. A well-designed organizational structure accomplishes the following:

*   Attracts the best people.

*   Builds their commitment to running their piece of the business as if it were there own.

*   Prevents conflicts of interests and other productivity-damaging hurdles.

*   Channels their efforts into teamwork rather than working in isolation.

*   Builds a culture of customer focus (internal and external).

*   Gets staff to focus on results (products) rather than efforts.

*   Clarifies to clients where to go for what.

Furthermore, the results of such an investment are enduring. An organizational structure based on the Building Blocks Approach can last a lifetime, evolving gracefully over time rather than periodically demanding radical changes in a zig-zag path to an unknown destination.

As new business problems arise, staff will implicitly know their respective roles in solving them. As the environment changes — adjustments to clients' organizational structure, business strategies, new technologies, or the degree of decentralization — the organization will automatically adapt without the need for significant restructurings.

With an organization that adapts flexibly within consistent, stable principles, one no longer needs to hear that plaintive cry, *"What, another reorganization!?"*

It's my hope that, as students of the science of structural design, a new breed of systematic executives will begin to sort out the organizational hurdles that get in the way of good people performing, and build organizations in which everyone can succeed.

Index